Collins

I SMIRT, YOU STOOZE THEY KRUMP...

J CROZIER C MCKEOWN & E SUMMERS

HarperCollins Publishers
Westerhill Road
Bishopbriggs
Glasgow G64 2QT

First Edition 2006
© HarperCollins Publishers 2006
www.collins.co.uk

ISBN-13: 978–0–00–721176–0
ISBN-10: 0–00–721176–7

Designed by Mark Thomson,
Morven Dooner
Typeset in Martin Majoor's FF Nexus
by Interactive Sciences Ltd,
Gloucester, England
Printed and bound by Legoprint SPA

ACKNOWLEDGEMENTS
We would like to thank those authors
and publishers who kindly gave
permission for copyright material
to be used in the Collins Word Web.
We would also like to thank Times
Newspapers Ltd for providing valuable
data. All rights reserved.

COMPILED BY: Justin Crozier, Cormac
McKeown

EDITED BY: Elspeth Summers

WITH THANKS TO: Jeremy Butterfield,
Andrew Holmes, Michael Munro,
Ruth Wajnryb

William Collins' dream of knowledge
for all began with the publication of
his first book in 1819. A self-educated
mill worker, he not only enriched
millions of lives, but also founded a
flourishing publishing house. Today,
staying true to this spirit, Collins
books are packed with inspiration,
innovation, and practical expertise.
They place you at the centre of a
world of possibility and give you
exactly what you need to explore it.

Language is the key to this
exploration, and at the heart of
Collins Dictionaries is language as it
is really used. New words, phrases,
and meanings spring up every day,
and all of them are captured and
analysed by the Collins Word Web.
Constantly updated, and with over
2.5 billion entries, this living language
resource is unique to our dictionaries.

Words are tools for life. And a Collins
Dictionary makes them work for you.

Collins. Do more.

Can You Still Speak English?

Blook? Brrreeeport? Crunk? Gemmelsmerch? Krump?
Dooced? Frankendoodle? Hyote? Gling? Grup?

If these words leave you stumped, then help is at
hand. *I Smirt, You Stooze, They Krump* is an essential
guide to the latest developments in the biggest,
brashest, and most exciting language in the world.
English is evolving – and mutating – faster than ever
before. Keeping up with these changes is quite a
challenge, and one that draws on all of Collins'
resources and expertise. But there's no denying that
it's also great fun. For glinting among the hoard of
new names for chemical compounds, recently
identified bacteria, and other workaday additions to
the language are those little nuggets of meaning
that make us smile. Sometimes it is because a word
represents an exciting new idea or discovery. Maybe
the term itself is inventive, funny, rude, or
controversial. Often it stands out because it sums
up, in a couple of syllables, the times we live in. This
book is a collection of such gems, unearthed in
Collins' various language monitoring programmes.
They have all been thoroughly researched and
presented in context, both in terms of how they are
used and where they fit into greater linguistic
trends.

New words enter our language in a variety of ways.
English is spoken worldwide, and is also the *lingua*

franca of the internet. This unique status means that in many places, English is rubbing shoulders with entirely different languages – and absorbing words directly from them. At the same time, its written forms are in constant flux on the internet. As a result, English now forms the basis of a huge range of overlapping and interlinked dialects, of which *Hinglish*, *leetspeak*, and that rather more established dialect, 'Standard English', are all examples. Words from other languages can move around this network at the speed of a broadband connection.

Other words and phrases, like *mobisode, pharmbot,* and *silent disco*, come into being because a new creation requires a new name. Technology is usually the driving force here – you can't have a silent disco without wireless headphones – and each week sees fresh inventions needing fresh words to describe them. Some will disappear almost as quickly as they arrived, but others are here to stay.

A further class of neologism reflects inventiveness with language rather than with technology. People are fundamentally playful; we love allusions, metaphors, and puns. Much of the new language we create each year is of this sort: *manscaping, smirting,* and *tanorexic*, for example.

Other words seem completely alien: *nang, sket*, and *Creps*. Terms like these function as code, allowing certain groups to keep their business secret from the outside world. Youth slang is the most obvious example of this; its constantly changing vocabulary is clearly designed to exclude parents and teachers from the conversation. It's hard to keep a secret, of course, and sooner or later the code breaks down. *Creps* and *nang* have had widespread media exposure recently, and have been robbed of their disguise, so there is a need for yet more in-words for the in-crowd.

And it's not just subcultures that add to our vocabulary. The media has a massive influence. TV and film scriptwriters create a common linguistic currency by giving us a wealth of catchphrases and neologisms to draw on – from *frenemy* to *sorbet sex* – and the internet reinforces this by allowing us to discuss our favourite entertainments endlessly.

Regardless of how they arrived, all the new words in this book are now part of our growing lexicon. How long each survives is another matter entirely. While they are here, though, let's celebrate them for the miniature snapshots of modern life they are.

I Smirt, You Stooze, They Krump examines the English language in the late noughties and finds it to be in rude health. Keep it handy if you like to have the last word: on society, from *asbomania* to *shoulder surfing*; politics, from *dog-whistling* to *slacktivism*; technology, from *bot herds* to *voice lifts*; and world language, from *biznismeni* to *vuvuzela*.

Justin Crozier, Cormac McKeown, Elspeth Summers

November 2006

HOW TO USE THIS BOOK

I Smirt, You Stooze, They Krump is designed with easy browsing in mind. Most of it is self-explanatory – you don't have to read the following to enjoy the book but here is some information to help you get the most out of it.

• Headwords

All main entries, including acronyms and abbreviations, are printed in boldface type and are listed in strict alphabetical order, with any common variant spellings given after the headword:

exergaming *or* **exertainment** *n.* the playing of ...

• Labels

The standard parts of speech are presented in labels preceding the sense or senses relating to that part of speech. Where one word can be used as more than one part of speech, the change is indicated by the symbol |

reboot *vb.* **1** to abandon ... | *n.* **2** a new version ...

A noun or interjection that is commonly used as if it were an adjective is labelled (*as modifier*):

wiki ... **3** *as modifier*: wiki technology

When a verb is limited to transitive use, it is labelled (*tr*); if it is intransitive only, it is labelled (*intr*). Absence of a label means the verb can be used both transitively and intransitively.

If a particular sense of a word is restricted as to appropriateness, connotation, subject field, region, etc, an italic label is given:

informal n. **1** an adult who is still …

• *Etymologies*

Etymologies are provided for any word whose origins are not immediately apparent (or at least unambiguously so), in square brackets after the definition. Parent words from which the headword is derived (and which you might expect to find in a large dictionary such as the *Collins English Dictionary: Complete and Unabridged*) are given in small capitals:

Andymonium *n.* *Brit informal* the frenzy of spectator and media … [c21: from Andy (Murray) + PANDEMONIUM]

• *Derivations*

Words derived from a headword by the addition of suffixes such as -ly, -ness, etc, are presented in boldface type after the etymology (or definition if there is no etymology). They are preceded by the symbol > and the meaning of each can be deduced from that of the relevant headword:

overclocking *n.* … [c21: …] > **overclocker**

• *Examples of use*

Every entry is supported by a citation (from a newspaper, magazine, website, broadcast, etc) illustrating both its currency and how it is used in today's English.

I Smirt, You Stooze, They Krump
A–Z

adultescent *informal n.* **1** an adult who is still actively interested in youth culture | *adj.* **2** aimed at or suitable for adultescents

> You are without serious commitments – no mortgage, no kids – and you live with your parents, so you have plenty of cash to spend on clothes, phones and music players. If that's a description of you, you're an adultescent (*Sunday Morning Herald*)

advergaming *n. internet* a method of interactive marketing in which free downloadable computer games appear on websites (often as pop-ups) to advertise a company or product [ADVER(TISING) + GAMING]

> To reach kids and teens to promote Disneyland's 50th anniversary this year, Walt Disney Co. will use one of the hottest – and most controversial – gimmicks in the media business: 'advergaming' (*USA Today*)

airboarding *n.* a sport in which participants hurl themselves headfirst down snow-covered slopes, lying flat on an inflatable board resembling a bodyboard > **airboard** *n, vb.* > **airboarder** *n.*

> They call it airboarding, and the device with the Lilo appearance more normally associated with the swimming pool is the latest thing in the snow sports world this winter (*The Times*)

ambush marketing *n.* the practice (by a company) of promoting itself at an event or competition of which it is not an official sponsor, for example by paying sportspeople to wear its logo, or distributing eye-catching branded merchandise to fans

> Dutch fans are being handed orange shorts to watch the Argentina World Cup match if they wear trousers promoting a beer which is not the official sponsor. Up to 1,000 fans had to watch Friday's game against Ivory Coast in their underpants after being denied entry because they were wearing the orange lederhosen. Fifa said a bid at 'ambush marketing' was not allowed (*BBC News*)

analogue *or sometimes US* **analog** *n. informal* a person who is afraid of using new technological devices. *Compare* **digital native, digital immigrant**

> Today, he says, some 70% of the world's population are 'analogues', who are 'terrified by technology', and for whom the pain of technology 'is not just the time it takes to figure out new gadgets but the pain of feeling stupid at each moment along the way' (*The Economist*)

Andymonium *n. informal* the frenzy of spectator and media excitement that surrounds the matches, particularly at Wimbledon, of Scottish tennis player

Andy Murray (born 1987) [from *Andy* (Murray) +
(PANDE)MONIUM, influenced by *Henmania*, similar
fervour surrounding English player Tim Henman
(born 1974)]

> British tennis' hottest property has been trying to
> keep a low profile, practising, listening to his iPod™
> and playing his Xbox™. But elsewhere it was chaos –
> or Andymonium – ahead of his third round match on
> centre court later today (*The Scotsman*)

Anthropocene *n.* a proposed term for the present
geological epoch (from the end of the 18th century
onwards), during which humanity has begun to have a
significant impact on the environment [from
ANTHROPO-, indicating man or human, + -CENE,
denoting a recent geological period. Coined by Paul J
Crutzen, a Nobel laureate in chemistry]

> Scientists are beginning to accept that Earth has
> entered a new geological epoch, the 'Anthropocene'.
> The EuroScience forum in Stockholm heard on
> Thursday that climate change was the most obvious of
> a complex range of man-made effects that is rapidly
> changing the physics, chemistry and biology of the
> planet (*The Financial Times*)

approximeeting *n.* *informal* the practice of a group of
people making indefinite plans to meet and then

altering those plans regularly via mobile phones
according to changing circumstances [a blend of
APPROXIMATE and MEETING]

> This [proliferation of mobile phones] has many
> implications, but the most common one, and perhaps
> the thing that has changed British culture for ever, is
> that of approximeeting. People no longer need to
> make firm plans about when and where to meet (*The
> Guardian*)

Arab street *n.* **the** *informal* public opinion in the
Arab world

> He has seen Lebanese protestors topple their puppet
> government without bloodshed. And he knows this is
> just a foretaste of things to come in the Middle East.
> Mr Jumblatt is no fool. He can see the so-called 'Arab
> Street' is no longer cheering the mullahs (*The Sun*)

asbomania *n.* *British, informal* the perceived
indiscriminate and excessive use by the authorities of
anti-social behaviour orders [from ASBO (anti-social
behaviour order) + -MANIA]

> Equally important, however, is the commissioner's
> piercing critique of 'asbomania' and the over-
> criminalisation of Britain's youth ... he fears the over-
> broad definition of antisocial behaviour, the fast-track
> to overcrowded prisons that Asbos have become and
> the vile and dangerous 'naming and shaming' of

youngsters in particular *(The Guardian)*

assvertising *n. informal* the use of advertising on the underwear of attractive young models who wear short skirts and contrive to display the corporate message by stooping to pick up dropped items, tying shoelaces, etc [from ASS (buttocks) + ADVERTISING]

> Assvertising – advertising on bikini underwear. Worn and flashed by female models on the street, the butt-borne billboards are designed to attract young male consumers. No doubt they do *(Wired)*

> Welcome, then, to the latest idea from maverick New York-based creative marketers NightAgency, which they teasingly call 'assvertising'. The concept is helpfully illustrated with a cartoon picture of a most comely looking woman, wearing a bikini, with one of those 'Your ad here' signs pointing to her bottom. As they point out, if it's the right bottom, all eyes are going to be there anyway, so why not send your logo along for the ride? *(The Guardian)*

astroturfing *n. politics* a PR tactic in which hired acolytes or paid employees are used to offer ostensibly enthusiastic and spontaneous grassroots support for a politician, business, etc [from ASTROTURF, a type of artificial grass]

> In America, they call it 'astroturfing': the faking of

grassroots support for a politician or a product whose popularity is on the slide. Now it emerges that a tactic invented by US pharmaceutical firms to promote drugs – and promptly adopted by the Republicans to shore up George Bush after 9/11 – was imported to Britain to help get Tony Blair re-elected (*The Guardian*)

autocasting *n.* a form of broadcasting in which text from a blog is automatically converted to audio files that can be downloaded as a podcast [from AUTO + (POD)CASTING]

Podcasts are generally voice broadcasts while autocasting is a speech-synthesized version of regular text blogs (*Digital Inspiration*)

babymoon *n.* **1** a luxurious or relaxing holiday for expectant parents **2** a holiday for parents and their newborn child [from BABY + (HONEY)MOON]

Babymoon marketers hope to ease some of the pain. [One company] in Los Cabos, Mexico, offers a four-night 'babymoon' package, from $2,322 to $12,122 per expectant couple. If they've already had the baby, the hotel can provide a tiny robe and slippers, a crib with a hypoallergenic mattress, and the all-important diaper pail (*US News.com*)

badonkadonk *n. US, informal* curvaceous female buttocks [imaginary onomatopoeia; from the imagined sound that such a posterior might make in motion]

> So, as a service to all of the professional athletes that read my columns, I'll leave you with a new possibility for a sports cliché… 'I tagged that fastball like it was a nice, round badonkadonk' (*The Stanford Daily*)

baile funk *n.* **1** a style of dance music from the favelas (or slums) of Brazil **2** a dance music event at which such music is played [from Portuguese 'funk ball']

> Originating in the slums of Rio de Janeiro in Brazil, the saucy rhythms of baile funk are about to invade the UK (*The Sun*)

Band-Aid baby *n. informal* a child conceived to strengthen a faltering relationship

> Weeks later, she announced she was pregnant. It was, the cynics said, a so-called 'Band-Aid baby' to patch up the marriage (*The Daily Mail*)

bandslash *n.* a type of imaginative erotic fiction (known as slash fiction) in which two or more popular musicians are cast as the protagonists [from BAND + SLASH (FICTION), so called because of the forward slash that typically separates the names of the lustful protagonists in the titles of such fanciful tales]

Even more amusing is that those doing the wishful humping in bandslash aren't your usual pin-ups. Bandslash has gone indie. This is a shadowy world where the boys in Franz Ferdinand are each others' fetish objects, and former Libertines Carl Barat and Pete Doherty, lovers (*The Guardian*)

barbecue stopper *n. Australian, informal* **1** a controversial current-affairs issue **2** a social gaffe [from the notion that such a discussion (or gaffe) is likely to interrupt a barbecue with loud debate (or shock)]

A new research project examining how family care and housework are shared between the sexes promises to be a barbecue stopper, says Sex Discrimination Commissioner (*headline from Independent Education Union (Australia) website*)

basbo *n. British, informal* an asbo applicable to children under the age of 10 [from B(ABY) + ASBO]

The 'Basbo' would be seen as a less harsh version of normal anti-social behaviour orders… It would mean a child could be barred from verbally abusing neighbours or from entering parts of an estate (*BBC Online*)

bashment *n.* a type of dance music fusing elements of house and ragga [from Jamaican dialect *bash* lively, exciting, etc, related to BASH party + -MENT suffix forming nouns, indicating state or quality]

> Playing video games is a popular pastime for the Hackney 15-year-olds, as is shopping in Wood Green, at Primark, New Look and Topshop, listening to rap and hip hop and bashment (*The Guardian*)

bastard pop *n. informal* a type of popular music in which two records, usually from different genres or eras, are blended together into a whole, often using the vocal performance from one and the instrumental from the other

> Despite the fact that bastard pop was born from sampling and internet file-swapping, the music industry has adopted a surprisingly laissez-faire attitude toward the movement. Some bands have gone the legal route and gotten clearance for mashed-up recordings (*The Globe and Mail*)

Beboer *n.* a user of the Bebo.com social-networking website [from BEBO a trademark + -ER]

> For such a small country, Ireland can claim a significant percentage of Beboworld, with company figures estimating that there are 500,000 Beboers in the Republic (*Sunday Independent*)

beck *n. British, informal, derogatory* a wealthy Jewish fashion-conscious teenager, esp one from North

London [of uncertain origin]

> The 20 women come from every strand of Jewish society. There are 'becks' (the north London tribe of moneyed teenagers closest to chavs) and the wife of the Israeli ambassador in London (*The Sunday Times*)

beigism *n. informal* a disparaging term for the conventional or conservative attitudes of suburbia and its resulting bland culture [from the colour BEIGE, when considered as bland and unexciting]

> As much as the book is about the founding of a newspaper, or a low-level media war in a foreign city, it's about both of the authors. It is about their escape, their self-imposed exile, their insecurities, their foibles. At times, the endearing whiff of self-deprecation becomes the stench of self-loathing. Their constant referral to college keg parties, or the BBQ morality of white middle-class America is a metaphorical thread running through every chapter. It says as much about their distaste for the 'beigism' of suburban America, as it does about fitting in (*cdi.org*)

Berliner *n.* a newspaper format, sized somewhere between a tabloid and a traditional broadsheet [because the format was first adopted by Berlin newspapers]

> The Berliner format, which is used by several mainland European titles, including *Le Monde,* had

never before been adopted by a national newspaper in the UK. Its introduction followed relaunches of *The Independent* and *The Times* as tabloid newspapers and left only two national broadsheet dailies *(The Guardian)*

bhangrage *n. music* a style of music fusing together elements of bhangra and garage

'Punjabnay' starts off as though it's typical bhangra but before long the bassline kicks in to turn this into a sweet piece of bhangrage complete with MCs spitting out their lyrics *(BBC)*

Big Pharma *n. informal* the world's large multinational pharmaceutical companies, viewed collectively

Beset by multiple ailments, Big Pharma needs a dose of newly patented miracle cures, drug industry experts say *(The Philadelphia Enquirer)*

bioart *n.* art that is inspired by biology, esp that which is created using techniques more usually associated with biological science

'Bioart' is becoming a force in the creative world. A glowing bunny made the front page of newspapers across the country two years ago, and installations that require biohazard committee approval are increasingly common at universities and art galleries *(Wired)*

The new web

For the last decade, the internet has been the major force in the generation and propagation of new language. It allows new words to spread almost effortlessly, and, as it develops, spawns the neologisms that are needed to describe its functions. The rise of **Web 2.0** indicates that this trend is set to continue.

Web 2.0 is the modish name given to the altered 'model' of the internet. Previously, the internet was somewhere you went to get information – in essence, a vast electronic library. While it still works in this way, its primary focus is shifting from a passive experience to an active one. Phenomena such as *wikis* and the **blogosphere** allow every internet user to air their opinions, with some bloggers even finding more permanent expression in the form of **blooks.** Thus the web is less a reference tool and more a hive of creative activity, eagerly embraced by **Generation C.**

The blogosphere has spawned new forms of journalism, often competing directly with the **lamestream** media, with online reporting from even the front line of war zones, as with **milblogs.** The power of the blog was demonstrated in the US in 2004 when CBS anchor Dan Rather was toppled by the **pajamahadeen,** zealous bloggers who checked the facts that the media professionals hadn't. There's an anarchic streak to the bloggers' creativity, as with the use of **brrreeeport** to subvert website rankings. But even the blogosphere is being colonized by the forces of commerce, as the emergence of **splogs** and **sping** demonstrate.

biznismen *n, pl.* **biznismeni** *derogatory* (in Russia) a person who became rich in the immediate post-communist era, usually through taking control of and then selling state-owned assets rather than through legitimate entrepreneurial activity [Russian, from plural of English BUSINESSMAN used as a singular]

> It is often difficult to tell a gangster from a
> 'biznismen' – a distinction, indeed, many within the
> Russian business class themselves see as irrelevant
> (*parliament.uk*)

black hat *n. computing* a hacker who uses his or her skills to malicious or criminal ends [on the analogy of old Western movies in which the baddies typically wore black hats]

> the FBI has identified the average black hat as 26 years
> old, white and male (*The Times*)

black site *n.* one of a number of sites outside the US, rumoured to be used for the interrogation and perhaps torture of prisoners by CIA operatives

> On Tuesday Rice will sign a deal opening American
> facilities in Romania that will provide stopover points
> for US missions in the Middle East and central Asia.
> One of them is likely to be the air force base of Mihail
> Kogalniceaunu, which has come under suspicion as an

alleged 'black site' (*The Times*)

bleachorexic *n.* a person with a compulsion to make their teeth whiter by bleaching them continually [from BLEACH + (AN)OREXIC]

> The country that inspired Austin Powers and his yellowing overbite is now experiencing a boom in teeth bleaching. Britain has seen a five-fold increase in people – dubbed 'bleachorexics' by worried dentists – demanding tooth-whitening procedures. This may be aesthetically pleasing. But now medical experts are warning that Britons in search of the perfect Hollywood smile risk permanent damage to their teeth, gums and even throats (*The Independent*)

bleg *informal n.* **1** a blog in which the author asks for donations | *vb.* **2** to use one's blog to ask for donations of money, goods, or esp technical assistance [from BL(OG) + (B)EG] > **blegging** *n.* > **blegger** *n.*

> Warning: I'm about to bleg. I want you to buy me a laptop (*TheAgitator.com*)

blogosphere *n. informal* the world's weblogs viewed collectively; the blogging world [from (WE)BLOG + SPHERE: the 'o' is added in imitation of *logosphere, stratosphere, atmosphere,* etc]

... it's refreshing to find almost as many left-wing bloggers as conservative ones these days, and there are many more whose politics defy easy characterisation. The range of voices in the blogosphere suggests that dissatisfaction with mainstream media is no longer an exclusive entitlement of the right (*The Age*)

blook *n.* a book derived from a blog or website [from BLO(G) + (BO)OK]

However easy blook publishing becomes, few blooks will become best-sellers… But then many bloggers don't aspire to the *New York Times'* best-seller list – sometimes making a blook for dad is good enough (*Business Week*)

bluebugging *n.* a form of mobile-phone hacking similar to bluesnarfing, but which allows the hacker to make calls (to premium-rate numbers, etc) from the mobile phone under attack [from BLUE(TOOTH) a trademark + BUGGING, possibly because the hacker can use the hacked phone to call his or her own phone without the owner's knowledge, thereby listening in to nearby conversations] > **bluebug** *vb.* > **bluebugger** *n.*

Let's say you and I are competing for a big contract with an oil company. I want to hear everything that happens in your meeting with the VP of Massive Oil Inc., so I hire a black-hat phreak to take over your cell

> phone. Once he's bluebugged it, I tell him to have
> your mobile call mine. The phone that's sitting in your
> jacket pocket is now picking up everything you and
> the VP say (*Wired*)

bluesnarfing *n.* the practice of using one Bluetooth™-enabled mobile phone to steal contact details, ringtones, images, etc. from another [from BLUE(TOOTH) a trademark + SNARF]

> Not only were we able to find out her name from the
> Nokia™ 6310 on the table beside her, we could have
> found out the names, phone numbers, e-mail and
> conventional mail addresses of all her friends and
> contacts stored on the handset. We could have found
> out where she was planning to go and whom she was
> planning to meet ... It's illegal under data protection
> legislation but, hey, who'd know? Welcome to the
> world of bluesnarfing (*The Times*)

Boden Man *n. British, politics* a relatively affluent middle-class man who is disaffected with Blairite Britain [from Boden, the catalogue clothes retailer supposedly favoured by middle-aged, middle-class men]

> Boden Man knows this is the modern world, but can't
> help thinking things are, to use a favourite expression
> of his, 'out of whack'. He remembers when Elton John
> was a naff, balding, bespectacled has-been; and fears

that this description might now apply to him (*The Independent*)

body-shading *n.* bodybuilding without the pain: a non-surgical cosmetic procedure in which areas of the body are painted with an airbrush to enhance – or simulate the existence of – muscle definition

> It is the latest in body-building regimes: no long hours in a sweaty gym, no calorie counting and as much fatty food as you want to eat. The big secret is: you cheat by airbrushing in your new physique. Body-shading has long been used by models and film stars. Now it is becoming widely available on the high street. With a bit of fake tan and a few patches of carefully darkened skin, almost anybody can have finely honed stomach muscles, a firm jaw line or cheekbones to die for (*The Times*)

bogoth *n. Australian, slang. Another word for* **gogan**

> I can't believe you had sex with a bogoth! Loser! (*LiveJournal Forum*)

bot herd *n.* a group of computers, infected with malign programs via the internet, that can be controlled remotely to, for example, mount denial-of-service attacks. *Also called* **bot army** [from (RO)BOT + HERD] > **bot herdsman** *n.*

> Like so much else in the world of computers and the

internet, this practice started out as relatively harmless fun among computer buffs. It was the age of 'bot rustling', a competition in which herdsmen would compete to try to seize the slave computers from their rival's bot herds. Soon, however, the bot herdsmen found organised criminals literally knocking on their doors (*The Guardian*)

botnet *n. sometimes with a capital* a network of computers infected by a program that communicates with its creator in order to send unsolicited e-mails, attack websites, etc [from (RO)BOT + NET(WORK)]

Recently we have seen a supply chain emerging. Botnet 'herders' will pay hackers for the botnets they have assembled. Such herds can then be sold to organised criminals for spamming and extortion purposes (*Computing Magazine*)

bouncebackability *n. informal* the ability to recover after a setback, esp in sport; resilience [coined in 2005 by the then Crystal Palace manager Iain Dowie (born 1965), it was used at first mostly in jokey references to sporting comebacks, but is now employed more generally]

[One trader] said: 'The Footsie is showing bouncebackability; it's very encouraging for bulls' (*The Economist*)

Word wars

Words, as the building blocks of language, are useful tools – and powerful weapons. This is especially true in the propaganda battles around actual warfare. The struggle for 'hearts and minds' has created a host of military euphemisms such as *collateral damage* and *friendly fire*. A recent example is **extraordinary rendition,** a phrase that been central to the debate over torture, along with the **ticking bomb scenario.**

But words have other offensive and defensive uses. The internet and the **blogosphere** have brought the power of a single word to the fore, as when Robert Scoble coined **brrreeeport** to enable bloggers to outwit the blog-ranking systems of the major search engines. This meaningless word quickly became one of the most popular search terms on the web.

An ingenious new approach is the creation and propagation of a word as a direct attack on someone else. After US senator Rick Santorum made controversial statements about homosexuality, gay sex columnist Dan Savage launched a campaign to associate Santorum's surname with something very unpleasant indeed. Savage's readers took up the idea, with the result that the word now appears on thousands of websites, and has been alluded to in respectable publications such as *The Economist*. We're likely to see more of this kind of 'word war' in the future, as **digital natives** and **Generation C** flex their online muscles.

brain fingerprinting *n.* a technique in which sensors worn on the head are used to measure the involuntary brain activity of someone in response to certain images or pieces of evidence pertaining to a crime

> Critics say brain fingerprinting would be ineffective in cases in which a person commits a crime while under the influence of alcohol or drugs. 'If your memory isn't functioning (because) you're stoned when you commit the crime, you're certainly not going to remember it the next day, let alone years later,' said J. Peter Rosenfeld, a psychology professor at the Institute for Neuroscience (*The Denver Post*)

bredren *n. British, youth slang* a close friend, companion [from Jamaican patois, from BRETHREN]

> Hey bredren, just got around to listening to some of your tracks and BOOM, you're killin' it! (*MySpace.com*)

BRICs *n acronym for* Brazil, Russia, India, and China: seen collectively as the most important emerging economies with large potential markets. *Compare* **Chindia**

> The brics – a new acronym in world affairs jargon – refers to Brazil, Russia, India and China. They are large in territory and resources, they are populous, and, says the Goldman Sachs team, they are on their way up (*The Australian*)

Britalian *adj.* of or relating to a version of Italian cuisine common in Britain, considered to lack authenticity and flavour [a blend of BRITISH and ITALIAN]

> First the curry fell victim to the British habit of taking liberties with a national cuisine. Now Italian food is being subjected to a form of culinary colonialism with the big supermarkets serving up a diet of 'Britalian' food that tastes nothing like the real thing, according to a leading Italian chef (*The Guardian*)

bro job *n. chiefly US, slang* an act of oral sex between two ostensibly heterosexual male friends, esp when under the influence of alcohol [from BRO (in the sense of a close associate) + (BLOW) JOB]

> Tales of the bro job have been whispered around these parts for months, although 'straight' men willing to own up to giving or getting one have been elusive (*The Phoenix*)

Brokeback marriage *n. informal* a marriage in which one of the partners is homosexual or has had a homosexual relationship in the past [from the 2005 film *Brokeback Mountain* (itself an adaptation of a short story of the same name by Annie Proulx), which depicts a gay relationship between two cowboys, both of whom have married women]

> I'm just discovering my marriage of 12 years
> (relationship of more than 20), is a Brokeback
> marriage. I've been the woman he had zero sexual
> interest in. His orientation is buried underneath a
> lifetime of denial… (*Nerve.com letters page*)

brown noise *or* **brown note** *n.* **1** *physics* a frequency
that resembles Brownian motion when its sound
signal is graphically represented **2** in urban myth, a
sound frequency that causes people to defecate
involuntarily [popularized by *South Park,* an irreverent
TV cartoon first broadcast in 1997]

> If the human body is subjected to low-frequency
> sound waves (between 10.5 and 16 Hz), there is often
> an uncontrollable and instant urge to defecate. While
> the use of this 'brown noise' has been investigated for
> military and crowd control uses, I've not found any
> references to its use as an anti-constipation device
> (*halfbakery.com*)

brrreeeport *n.* *internet* a word inserted by bloggers
somewhere within their blogs to draw attention to
their websites, and subvert the ranking order used by
major internet institutions (because the high-profile
inventor of the term succeeded in generating
widespread interest in it, prompting many web users

to include it in their internet searches) [coined by blogger and Microsoft employee Robert Scoble]

> Bloggers are striking back at the dominance of the main search engine companies, Google, Microsoft and Yahoo!, by adding the word 'brrreeeport' to their sites. It appears to be catching on: according to Technorati, the internet-monitoring site, brrreeeport was the most searched-for term on the internet yesterday (*The Times*)

bumping *n. informal* the practice of making a job redundant but keeping on the person who did that job and offering them the job of another employee whose dismissal would have a smaller financial impact on the employer

> For most people, any experience of 'bumping' will be confined to volatile airport queues where the airline is desperately trying to persuade passengers to give up their seats on an overbooked flight ... But bumping is taking on a more prominent role in the thorny area of redundancy and unfair dismissal law and has highlighted the lengths employers need to go to to offer alternative employment when they are considering redundancies, if they are to avoid unfair dismissal claims against them (*Scotland on Sunday*)

Burberry ape *n. British, derogatory slang* an uncouth working-class British male, esp one with thuggish tendencies [a play on BARBARY APE + Burberry (a trademark), a fashion house allegedly favoured by such people]

> 'I wasn't doing anything and he just hit me with his truncheon.' How many times have you heard that from a Burberry ape limping home from an England match? (*The Bristol Evening Post*)

butt bra *n. chiefly US and Canadian* an undergarment for supporting the buttocks

> Don't laugh – she's already sold over 25,000 units at a cool $30 per butt bra. I should have seen this coming. There are surgical implants for just about everything, so it only makes sense that someone would come up with a non-surgical alternative. I guess working out just isn't fashionable any more (*The Asian Reporter*)

butters *adj. British, slang* (of a person) very ugly [perhaps shortened from 'butt ugly']

> And what of the ghastly phrase by which teenage boys refer to an ugly girl. No longer is she 'manky' or 'a minger', apparently. No, now she's 'butters'. Pronounced 'bu'ers', of course (*The Times*)

cakeage *n. Australian, informal* a charge levied in a restaurant for serving cake (such as a birthday cake) brought in from outside the premises [modelled on CORKAGE]

This from the city of the $45 main course … a group of diners at a birthday bash in Bondi were given the okay to bring in a cake but the waiter failed to mention there would be a $3 a person 'cakeage' charge. The total was $36 in cakeage – which was a bit rich given the mud cake cost only $20 (*The Courier-Mail*)

camera surfer *n. British, informal* a motorist who habitually exceeds the speed limit but who avoids triggering conventional speed cameras by slowing down to observe the limit while driving past them > **camera surfing** *n.*

The average speed camera scheme being trialled in Camden, north London, and also Belfast, is aimed at 'camera surfers' (*The Evening Times*)

camera tossing *n.* a method of creating unusual photographic images which involves setting a long exposure time on a camera, releasing its shutter, and tossing it in the air

Over the past few months … photographers around the world have embraced the hobby of 'camera tossing' as the hottest trend in digital imaging. By spinning a camera in the air – and, ideally, catching it afterwards – practitioners are surprising themselves with the abstract patterns of light serendipitously captured on their memory cards (*The Times*)

The linguistic revolution will be televised ...

Television is a constant presence in our lives, and, for most of us, constitutes much of the spoken word that we encounter each day. It's unsurprising, therefore, that TV wields a powerful influence over our language. In particular, long-running TV shows with well-established character and catchphrases have become part of our common culture, allowing us to allude in a word or phrase to a complex set of images and emotions.

American culture has had a substantial impact through the small screen: *The Simpsons* is probably the most *cromulent* example here. The antics of the four-fingered folk have *embiggened* our vocabulary with pungent phrases and vivid neologisms ranging from *cheese-eating surrender monkeys* to *craptacular*.

Friends has also had a remarkable influence on how many of us speak. To *go commando* is understood by many of us, and *Friends* has added a new speech pattern with its idiosyncratic use of *so* as in *that is so not my motto*. And *Sex and the City* has bequeathed us **frenemy** and **sorbet sex.**

Meanwhile, UK TV programmes have been exerting a powerful influence of their own. It's now virtually impossible to talk about your *local shop* without invoking images of incest and murder thanks to *The League of Gentlemen*, while *Little Britain* has given us *yeah-but-no-but* and *computer says no*, as well as lending *lady* connotations of unconvincing transvestism.

Cameroon *n. British, informal* a supporter of David Cameron, leader of the British Conservative Party from 2005

> Greeting him was a lone cheerleader, 54-year-old Anne Bond, heavily outnumbered by a dozen young 'Cameroons' from Leicester and Nottingham Student Tory Association (*The Telegraph*)

camwhore *slang n.* **1** a person who performs sexual or titillating acts in front of a webcam for the gratification of online customers who reward them with money or gifts | *vb.* **2** to perform such acts in return for money or gifts [from (WEB)CAM + WHORE]

> Like everything else in the insular webcam community, the meaning and morality of the wish lists is hotly debated by the cam kids themselves. Are you a 'camwhore' if you put up a wish list? If you don't show your tits, does that mean you're not 'whoring for hits'? What if you put up a wish list, but don't show skin? (*Salon.com*)

cankles *pl n. informal* thick or chubby ankles and lower calves [from CA(LF) + (A)NKLES, because it is supposedly impossible to determine where one ends and the other begins]

My cankles are so bad I have to buy knee socks once a month because the elastic stretches out in them. I'm thinking of taking viagra because my ankles have me so self conscious in the moments of intimacy that it's hard for me to focus on the task at hand (*HealthAndFitnessForums.Com*)

capper *n.* a person who records a television show and then illegally makes it available for people to download on the internet [of uncertain origin]

TV programmes can be watched through a computer with a TV tuner card, available at any computer store. Organised groups of 'cappers' in the US record shows when they are first broadcast and place high-quality files on the internet. Broadcasters and television production companies are about to begin prosecuting the 'cappers', and are expected to take steps to protect their programmes from piracy by offering the latest episodes of shows for download around the world for a small fee as soon as they are broadcast (*The Guardian*)

carbage *n.* *informal* **1** snack food that is of limited nutritional value but low in carbohydrates **2** a term used by overenthusiastic proponents of low-carb dieting to describe carbohydrates in general [from CARB(OHYDRATE) + (GARB)AGE]

… uniformly awful-tasting carbage – chips, cookies, candy bars, and other snacks – marketed to people on low-carbohydrate diets (*Wired*)

> I have a 15-year-old daughter who is LowCarbing with me, and even with me preparing her food it is a challenge around her friends … They are all skinny minnies who can eat 'carbage' all day long and never gain an ounce (*LowCarbFriends.com*)

carbon footprint *n.* a measure of the amount of carbon dioxide released into the atmosphere by a single endeavour or by a company, household, person, etc, through day-to-day activities over a given period (usually one year)

> I've now spent a month trying to reduce the so-called carbon footprint of my home. I've been on my hands and knees taping up my windows, I've insulated part of the roof, put in energy saving bulbs and turned down the thermostat. But the most significant thing I have done took just a couple of minutes – I timed it – and I didn't even raise a sweat. What I did will reduce the carbon emissions from the electricity I use to zero – I switched to a green electricity supplier (*BBC Newsnight*)

card tart *n.* *informal* a credit-card holder who continually changes providers, transferring their balance to another provider (offering a similarly low interest rate) whenever the agreed period of low interest on the prior loan is about to expire

[One] debt-dodging Yorkshire mum is a self-confessed 'card tart' and refuses point-blank to allow credit card companies to make a profit out of her. 'I'm proud to be a card tart,' she said. 'I use the facilities offered to me by credit card companies to my advantage' (*This Is York*)

celebreality *n.* a television genre that is unscripted and involves either the day-to-day documentation of a celebrity's life or competitive challenges that a celebrity or celebrities must perform [a blend of CELEBRITY and REALITY TV]

I will not pepper my conversation with references to celebreality shows. I will not mention Jodie Marsh being the most tragic thing on TV since the boy who gave birth to his twin. I will not even be aware of some young man-meat aged 16 called Richard Fleeshman who I would love to make my toy-boy bitch. From this day, I shall watch things like Panorama (is it even still on?) and *Newsnight*. (*popjustice.com*)

celebutante *n. informal* a well-off young woman who is a relative newcomer to fashionable society and who has achieved celebrity status [from CEL(EBRITY) + (DE)BUTANTE]

Paris Hilton is out with the music video for her first single, 'Stars are Blind'. The video, directed by Chris

Applebaum, shows everybody's favorite celebutante dressed in a teeny leopardskin bikini and frolicking along the beach with a hunky male model (*CBS News*)

celebutard *n.* *informal*, *derogatory* a celebrity noted for displays of stupidity [from CELEBU(TANTE) + (RE)TARD]

> Will Paris Hilton ever learn? When the celebutard was questioned under oath in the $10 million slander suit brought against her by jewelry heiress Zeta Graff, Hilton said Graff was as old as her mother 'and should stay at home with her child instead of being at nightclubs with young people. And just that… What else did I say? Just that she is not cute at all' (*The New York Post*)

chav bop *n.* *British*, *informal* a disco or party at which participants adopt clothing associated with the working-class youths popularly designated as 'chavs'; such clothing includes tracksuits, chequered baseball caps, white trainers, and ostentatious jewellery

> …the so-called 'chav bop' – a disco where you dress up as a working-class person – is an immovable fixture not only at public schools, but also throughout Oxford's colleges. Google the phrase and you receive … predictable snaps of well-bred young men, with captions like 'Rock 'ard', mugging for the camera using poses they have presumably learned from Goldie Lookin' Chain videos (*The Guardian*)

Chavian flu

A word that has had a spectacular impact on British English in recent years is *chav*, which has spawned a legion of derived terms. The word *chav* itself is far from new. It derives from the Romany *chavi*, meaning 'boy' or 'child', and, as *chav* or *chavvy*, has hovered on the fringes of English for a century or more, in dialect in various parts of the UK.

But what *is* new about *chav* is the way in which it has leapt from regional dialect to mainstream English through the internet. In the language of the web, *chav* has 'gone viral'. The 'chavian flu' that has gripped newspapers and blogs over the last couple of years may testify to our snobbery. But it's also proof of our love of word-play, through punning, rhyming, and allusion. *Chav*, as a short and distinctive monosyllable, is a perfect building block for a host of new words. Thus we have *chavian, chavtastic, chavalry, chavitude*, and even *chaveller's cheques* (dole payments). *Chavs* and *chav-nots* alike, we play *chavball*, pay *chavtaxes*, and read *chav lit* . And some of us may already be doffing our baseball caps to the *chavistocracy*.

Chav has already gone through some noticeable shifts in meaning. When it first exploded online, the word was used almost exclusively to indicate a specific sort of young hooligan, equivalent to the Scottish *ned* or the Northern Irish *spide*. It was then applied to those who dress in the tracksuited and baseball-capped fashion influenced by US hip-hop, before being used more generally still to denote anyone who demonstrates a lack of taste or refinement.

chessboxing *n.* a physically and mentally challenging sport in which participants contest alternating rounds of chess and boxing, of four and two minutes respectively, beginning and ending with chess (unless a participant is knocked out)

> Velcro rips. Amok slides back into his Everlast gloves, bites down on his mouthpiece, dances along the ropes. His king's in trouble, and his punches couldn't knock lint off a jacket. Stoldt floats toward him like a cloud of big hurt. Such is the bewildering beauty of chessboxing... (*Los Angeles Times*)

Chindia *n.* *informal* China and India considered together in terms of economic power and strategic importance. *See also* **BRICs** [from CH(INA) + INDIA]

> Chindia, where the world's workshop meets its office... The 'Chindia' region's potential of huge domestic markets – encompassing a third of humanity – cheap highly skilled labour and governments pursuing capital-friendly policies have led many to conclude that the world is at a tipping point in history (*The Guardian*)

chipmunking *n.* *informal* **1** the practice of continuously using one's PDA or similar handheld device during a meeting or while engaged in another public activity **2** a phenomenon whereby audio files (esp those accessible on the internet) play back faster than they should, resulting in high-pitched music, speech, etc, often to comical effect **3** (in eating competitions) the illicit practice of hiding uneaten food in the mouth, esp in the space between the teeth and the cheeks [(sense 1) Because the activity supposedly lends one the appearance of a chipmunk using its paws, for example, to shell a nut. (sense 2) From the high-pitched singing of various animated representations of chipmunks. (sense 3) From the stereotypical image of a chipmunk's bulging cheeks while feeding]

> The rules for the first annual Yale Angler's Journal Swedish fish-eating contest were mostly practical: One: 25 fish per person per round, must be consumed fully in one minute. Two: No chipmunking (that is, hiding fish in your cheeks). Three: No deliberate puking, and as for inadvertent puking, make it clean (*Yale Daily News*)

coasterize *vb.* to ruin a CD, esp while attempting to burn music, etc, onto it, thus rendering it useful only as a drinks coaster

> coasterize, verb: the word used in her office, Erica Bower informed us, for the process of turning a blank

recordable CD into an object useful only for resting drinks on. We were amused, and out of interest did a Google search to see if the term was also used elsewhere. It is indeed, so much so that if it hasn't already been pencilled in for [inclusion in] the dictionary, it will be any time now. Isn't language wonderful? (*New Scientist*)

computainment *n.* the use of personal computers for the purposes of entertainment [blend of COMPUTER and ENTERTAINMENT]

With the best-ever sharpness and brightness, high-resolution performance and a big screen that displays more without scrolling, this great Real Flat CRT 109B60 delivers an exciting, vibrant computainment experience (*smarter.com*)

consumer evangelist *n.* a consumer, particularly one in a position of respect in the community, who recommends a particular product to other consumers. *See also* **pyromarketing** [the word EVANGELIST is used to reflect the religious associations of the pyromarketing phenomenon]

Rather than promoting people and goods through mass-market media such as television, pyromarketing relies on 'consumer evangelists' who spread the word among like-minded people (*The Economist*)

copyfight 1 *n.* the conflict between copyright holders and individuals over the use, distribution, and replication of copyright materials **2** | *vb.* to engage in such a dispute [blend of COPYRIGHT and FIGHT] > **copyfighter** *n.*

> Unfortunately most of the copyfighters take the US view of copyright as entirely about economics, and neither understand nor are interested in moral rights (*BBC News*)

cotton-wool generation *n.* *informal* the children and teenagers of today, viewed as having been over-protected while growing up [from the practice of wrapping fragile things in cotton wool for protection]

> Driven to school, picked up from school, kept off the dangerous streets and away from the dangerous parks, they are the cotton-wool generation and, often, the only physical exercise they get is when their parents have time to supervise (*The Australian*)

creps *pl n.* *British, youth slang* trainers [of uncertain origin]

> I seen some cool Nikes but they looked like some stepped-up version of the ones on my feet (few added colours and lines), I seen some Reeboks (but everyone had them), then I seen the Cons (MY FACE LIT UP). They looked like some superstar creps on the shelf

with two big white stars, one on each side, around the
star was a raindrop shaped netting (*dooyoo.co.uk*)

crockumentary *n. informal* a pejorative term for a
documentary film whose accuracy and impartiality one
wishes to dispute [from CROCK (*of shit*) +
(DOC)UMENTARY]

> In the past, Hollywood has seldom risked box office
> take by producing message movies. But this election
> cycle's releases include not just the Bush-ripping
> crockumentary *Fahrenheit 9/11*, but a Halliburton-
> themed remake of *The Manchurian Candidate* and the
> forthcoming John Sayles film *Silver City*, the plot of
> which revolves around a grammar-garbling Western
> pol[itician] put up for office by nefarious corporate
> honchos (*The New York Times*)

crunk *n. music* a form of hip-hop originating in the
southern states of the USA [contraction of 'crazy
when drunk']

> In the US, Ciara is known as the First Lady of Crunk
> (*The Sun*)

cuddlecore *chiefly US and Canadian, informal n.* **1** a
type of up-tempo pop music influenced by punk but
characterized by gentler lyrics and more melodic
singing than are commonly associated with that

musical genre | *adj.* **2** of or relating to this style of music [from CUDDLE + (HARD)CORE]

> Known for the cutesy, 'cuddlecore' style of fun and bubbly garage pop, British Columbia group Cub released an album that affirmed they were capable of writing music with a little bit more depth and substance. Although it still sounds like the kind of music you want to listen to while driving around town in a convertible (*girliesogroovie.com*)

cyberathlete *n.* a professional player of computer games > cyberathletics *pl n.*

> At 21, the Kansas City man better known to computer buffs as 'Fatal1ty' has become the world's highest-paid video-gamer and a pioneer in a new branch of professional sport. The so-called cyberathlete, who has not worked at any other job since he left high school, has earned almost $150,000 (£105,000) over the past 2 years as he has 'out-fragged' competitors on the growing video-gaming circuit, which may one day rival tennis or golf (*The Times*)

cyberchondria *n.* *informal* hyperchondria fuelled by referring constantly to online sources, often resulting in misdiagnosis [from CYBER- + (HYPO)CHONDRIA] > cyberchondriac *n.*

> Doctors blame the wealth of web-based information for a rise in 'cyberchondria'. They claim many patients make their own incorrect self-diagnosis after reading

about conditions and then seek treatment they do not
need (*The Courier-Mail*)

Cyber Monday *n. US, informal* the Monday following
the Thanksgiving Holiday in the US, during which
workers are alleged to use their office high-speed
internet links for Christmas shopping [coined by the
National Retail Federation in the US, allegedly as a
marketing gimmick]

> It's a new phenomenon called 'Cyber Monday'. On
> November 28th millions of Americans returned to
> work after the Thanksgiving holiday and fired up their
> office computers to take advantage of high-speed
> internet links and continue the arduous task of
> hunting for Christmas presents (*The Economist*)

cybernym *n.* **1** a word, abbreviation, or acronym used
in computing **2** a pseudonym used on the internet [a
blend of CYBER- and -ONYM (combining form
indicating a name or word)]

> 'We are hackers and love to destroy Windows
> systems,' wrote a pair of virus-jugglers who go by the
> cybernyms of Circuit Breaker and Antimicro
> (*westword.com*)

daisy-chaining *n. British, slang* any group sexual
activity, esp among underage children

If a daisy-chaining session starts and one of the group does not want to be there, with peer pressure and the ignorance bred by our sex education classes what are the chances of them being able to say no? (*The Mirror*)

dark tourism *n.* tourism to sites associated with tragedy, disaster, and death

You can go on tours of Auschwitz. You can tour the slums of Rio or Siberian gulags. The academic literature on dark tourism argues that there can be good and ethical outcomes from this strange pastime. A frequently mentioned case in point is Auschwitz, which is falling apart and could use the tourist dollars for repair. Or in the case of the Rio slums, one could return home with a renewed intention to do something about poverty at home (*The Australian*)

data smog *n. informal* electronic information in the form of emails, text messages, links to websites, etc, presented for someone's attention but considered as a hindrance to concentration or relaxation

Data smog is a term coined by David Shenk to refer to the information overload that many of us have experienced recently. The internet allows us to have access to entire libraries of information. The sheer volume of information which many of us are exposed to every day may actually impair our performance and add stress to our lives (*mentalhealth.about.com*)

declinology *n.* the advocacy of the belief that one's

society is in decline [from DECLIN(E) + OLOGY]
> **declinologist** *n.*

> Declinology is the new dandyism. They have brought
> in a new attitude, which until now had spared the
> French: self-hatred. The declinologists don't speak
> about 'la crise' – that is much too lame. What they are
> talking about, and secretly dreaming of, is a national
> cataclysm (*The Guardian*)

deep Web *n.* the data stored on websites that is not
accessible through ordinary search methods, for
example the information that exists in searchable
databases that can be obtained only through queries

> The deep Web is the fastest-growing category of new
> information on the internet. According to this paper
> [The Deep Web White Paper], information on the
> deep Web is currently 400 to 550 times larger than the
> commonly defined World Wide Web. The Deep Web
> contains 7500 terabytes of information compared
> with 19 terabytes of information in the surface Web
> (*The Courier-Mail*)

dermaplaning *n.* a cosmetic treatment, often used to
treat acne scars, in which surface irregularities are
surgically scraped to give the skin a smoother
appearance [from Greek *derma* skin + PLANE]

> At £100 a session, face shaving, or dermaplaning as it's
> better known, is actually a skin-improving treatment,

where the top layers of skin are scraped off with a Teflon-coated blade to lessen irregularities and stimulate collagen growth. It might sound frightening, but benefits are said to include a younger-looking, more radiant and blemish-free complexion *(The Scotsman)*

digital immigrant *n. informal* a person who first became familiar with information technology as an adult. *Compare* **digital native, analogue**

...'digital immigrants' may not have noticed, but young 'digital natives' increasingly get their news from web portals such as Yahoo! or Google, and from newer web media such as blogs *(The Economist)*

digital native *n. informal* a person who has been familiar with information technology since childhood. *Compare* **digital immigrant, analogue**

In the meantime, wouldn't it be nice if producers of high-tech items remembered not all of us are digital natives and produced goods that do what we need them to do instead of making them so complex that often even tech experts have trouble with them? *(Bizjournals.com)*

disemvowel *vb. informal* to remove the vowels from a word in a text message, email, etc in order to abbreviate it [from DISEM(BOWEL) + VOWEL]

> The tendency seems irreversible. Broadsheet newspapers go tabloid, recognising the scarce elbowroom available to crushed commuters … In our impatience, we disemvowel language when we transmit terse txt msgs to our m8s, using punctuation marks and parentheses to semaphore our moods. We live in a culture suicidally intent on abbreviation (*The Observer*)

distorian *n. informal, derogatory* a historian who presents as fact a version of history they know to be inaccurate, esp to support an existing theory, advance a political cause, etc [from a blend of D(ISTORTION) and (H)ISTORIAN]

> We showed that every one – not many, not most, but all – of David Irving's claims were complete rot. They were based on lies, distortions and fabrications… Irving has been dubbed by some people on the internet as a 'distorian' (*The Jewish Tribune*)

dog-whistle *adj.* **1** relating to the targeting of potentially controversial messages to specific voters while avoiding offending those voters with whom the message will not be popular *dog-whistle politics* | *vb.* **2** to employ this kind of political strategy [from the fact that a dog whistle operates at frequencies that can be heard only by dogs. The phrase originated in

Australia, but became widespread in Britain during the 2005 General Election. It is associated with Lynton Crosby, an Australian political campaign director who worked for the British Conservative Party and who previously employed the technique in elections in his own country] > **dog-whistling** *n.*

> Costello cannot do what Howard's detractors describe as the dog-whistle stuff – sending out the subliminal, fear-driven messages on race and social change. (*The Age*)

dooced *adj. chiefly US, slang* dismissed from one's employment because of what one has written on a website or blog [from *www.dooce.com,* the web address of the first person to experience this]

> Recently Natalie was 'dooced' – fired after writing something about her job on a web log – just before Christmas, and she was flat broke. But her fans gave a lot of sympathy. Over the years some have even sent her marriage proposals. Voting has closed and next month Natalie will find out whether putting her life story on the web will be rewarded with a coveted Bloggie, the online equivalent of an Oscar. There's a hitch. Natalie Bizgirl is really James Guthrie, of Wellington, married with children and (last time we checked) a bloke (*Sunday Morning Herald*)

drink-dialling *n. informal* the inadvisable practice of making a phone call while drunk, esp to someone about whom one has romantic notions [modelled on DRINK-DRIVING]

> Beware the perils of drink-dialling: a friendly warning for a new student generation about the demon drink, mobile phones and old lovers (*The Times*)

drive-dialler *n. chiefly British* a person using a mobile phone that is not modified for safe in-car use while driving [modelled on DRINK-DRIVER] > **drive-dialling** *n.*

> When confronted with research showing that a motorist is four times more likely to cause an accident if he is talking on the phone, determined drive-diallers will turn prickly and claim persecution. 'Why don't they fine smokers/arguing couples/people picking their noses? They don't always have both hands on the wheel, they whinge, like junkies defending a filthy habit (*The Times*)

droplifting *n.* an artistic endeavour that involves surreptitiously leaving items that one has created or altered on shop shelves unbeknownst to the staff, to bring them to the attention of customers who may then attempt to purchase them [a blend of DROP + (SHOP)LIFTING]. *Also called* **shopdropping** *or* **reverse**

shoplifting > droplift *vb.*

> The practice is known as reverse shoplifting, or
> droplifting... Remember the Barbie Liberation
> Organisation, which swapped the voice boxes of
> hundreds of Teen Talk Barbies with those removed
> from Talking Duke GI Joe action figures? They were
> returned to toy-shop shelves, so that US Army hunks
> declared, 'I love shopping' and Mattel's blonde bimbos
> screamed: 'Vengeance is mine!' (*The Times Magazine*)

duvet diet *n.* a proposed method of maintaining a
healthy weight by sleeping longer, working on the
theory that the sleep-deprived body produces more
cortisol and less leptin, hormones that increase and
reduce appetite respectively

> Vivienne Parry, a former host of BBC's *Tomorrow's
> World* claims the 'duvet diet' could cut around 100
> calories out of your food intake every day simply by
> sleeping for an extra hour each night. Kept up for a
> year, that could equate to a weight loss of around
> 10lbs (*The Scotsman*)

dykon *n. informal* a celebrity idolized by lesbians
[from DYK(E) + (IC)ON]

> From icon to dykon: ever since she lifted off her
> welding mask in *Flashdance*, Jennifer Beals has been a
> pin-up for feisty women (*The Guardian*)

ecopod *n.* a coffin specially designed to be

environmentally friendly [from ECO- + POD]

> Ecopod creator Hazel Selena spent 10 years perfecting her 'green' coffin, which is based on ancient Egyptian caskets, using reclaimed materials and natural varnishes. Her design couldn't be more of a contrast to the usual chipboard variety, coated with faux-wood laminates, which represent 89 per cent of all coffins. Chipboard degrades slowly, leaking formaldehyde and glues into ground water and general water supplies, or emitting poisonous gases into the air (*The Guardian*)

edit war *n. informal* a dispute between two or more editors of an online open-source reference resource, in which the participants repeatedly edit the contributions of others to accord with their own views

> If you approach Wikipedia articles in a confrontational manner, then of course you will run into conflicts and edit wars. How else could it be, if people from all parts of the political, scientific and religious spectrum have to work together? (*slashdot.org*)

egocasting *n.* the practice, enabled by the rise of media sources that can be personalized, of allowing oneself to be exposed only to art, literature, music, comment, etc that one already knows to be to one's taste [from EGO + (BROAD)CASTING]

With the advent of TiVo™ and iPod™, however, we have moved beyond narrowcasting into 'egocasting' – a world where we exercise an unparalleled degree of control over what we watch and what we hear. We can consciously avoid ideas, sounds, and images that we don't agree with or don't enjoy (*The New Atlantis*)

elbow bump *n.* a proposed replacement for the traditional handshake, intended to be less conducive to communicable disease

Elbow bump. No, that isn't the latest type of punch from the National Hockey League or Ultimate Fighting. It's the way that the World Health Organization would like us to greet each other from now on. Yep, the handshake is seen as too efficient a way to spread disease – germs go from their nose, to their hands, to your hands to your nose and eyes – yuck! (*ABC News*)

electronic footprint *n.* *computing* data that identifies a computer that has connected to a particular website

In our digital work environment, a company or employee indulging in illegal or immoral activity is likely to have left a few electronic footprints. And it's a trail not easily erased. Deleting computer files only removes them from view, says company IT forensics specialist Daniel Ayers, it doesn't destroy them (*The New Zealand Herald*)

electronic ink *n.* a material consisting of microscopic

cells that can be turned from white to black and vice versa with the application of a small electric charge, allowing electronically stored text to appear on a paper-like substance

> Electronic ink can be printed on any surface, including walls, billboards, product labels and T-shirts. Homeowners could soon be able to instantly change their digital wallpaper by sending a signal to the electronic ink painted on their walls. … Another advantage electronic ink has over traditional computer displays is its readability. It looks more like printed text, so it's a lot easier on the eyes (*howstuffworks.com*)

email bomb *n. informal* a type of malicious internet action in which the perpetrator sends the victim (usually a company) a huge number of emails at once to overload its email systems

> Imagine the 'Unabomber' penning the script of *You've Got Mail*. An innocuous-looking mail knocks at your inbox, and boom! Thank your stars: the new scare doing the rounds, the email bomb, is lethal only in a virtual way (*Business Today*)

energy obesity *n. informal* the condition or quality of being wasteful of energy in the form of electricity, fossil fuels, etc, in one's day-to-day life

The Energy Saving Trust has revealed that the UK is in the grip of an 'energy obesity' epidemic. Households are set to waste about 750 million tonnes of carbon dioxide by 2020 unless everyone reduces energy levels in the home (*The Telegraph*)

evil twin *n.* a hidden wireless internet access point posing as a nearby legitimate one (as is commonly offered in cafés, airports, etc), but which is actually used by cybercriminals to divert sensitive information such as account numbers and passwords

Coffee shop Web surfers beware: An evil twin may be lurking near your favorite wireless hotspot (*USA Today*)

exergaming *or* **exertainment** *n.* the playing of video games that require rigorous physical exercise and are intended as a work-out, such as those in which players race a virtual bicycle on-screen by pedalling a simulator resembling an exercise bike [a blend of EXERCISE and GAMING as in the playing of a COMPUTER GAME]

Over half of Americans don't get enough exercise (now pegged at 30 minutes to an hour a day), and a quarter of us are total taters. But – get this – what if playing video games did provide some exercise? Some do! It's a new trend called 'exergaming' or 'exertainment'. The jam-packed hit of this year's

Consumer Electronics Show was a 'Cardio PlayZone,' featuring some of the new workout and movement video contraptions (*Fox News*)

exhibition killing *n.* the murder of a hostage by terrorists, filmed for broadcasting on television or the internet

> We should not broadcast images, appeals and statements that clearly vindicate the Nazi-like criminality of men like Zarqawi. Just the bald facts of the case and nothing more. We must stop being naive accomplices to exhibition killings (*The Guardian*)

extraordinary rendition *n.* the process by which a country seizes a person assumed to be involved in terrorist activity and then transports them for interrogation in a country where due process of law is unlikely to be respected

> Extraordinary rendition became frequent after the 11 September attacks. Egypt is the most common destination, but suspects have also been sent to Syria, Morocco and Jordan (*The Belfast Telegraph*)

fanon *n. informal* notions about the setting or characters in a work of fiction that do not arise from the original author, but rather from assumptions by fans [FAN + (CAN)ON]

Some of the presentations are scholarly and sedate, analyzing the books in the context of heroic myth. And then there are the fans, and they are legion, for whom the canon is only a jumping-off point. The other half of this conference is all about the fanon. The term refers to the burgeoning world of *Harry Potter* fan fiction (*The Globe and Mail*)

fattitude *n.* a positive attitude displayed by an overweight person towards their own body [a blend of FAT and ATTITUDE]

A spokesperson with 'fattitude' (in her own words), [she] not only defies but destroys all the stereotypical traits associated with larger ladies. Not afraid to speak her mind and proudly wearing a 'Fat is the New Black' T-shirt, she has already proven herself to be an inspiring alternative to the more commonly viewed women's lifestyle representatives (*rainbownetwork.com*)

fauxmosexual *n. informal* a heterosexual man who adopts fashion and mannerisms traditionally associated with homosexuality to gain social advantage, esp to become acquainted with women [FAUX + (HO)MOSEXUAL]

For every straight boy turned into a fauxmosexual with the flick of a camp wrist on television, there are at least two gay boys turning straight and coming out as football fans (*The Guardian*)

Science fiction, science fact

Sci-fi writers have had an unusual influence on the English language. There is a whole class of words that existed in science fiction before the real world caught up. The single best example of this is *cyberspace*, coined by William Gibson in his novel *Neuromancer* about a decade before the internet arrived. Czech writer Karel Capek gave many languages the word *robot* in his 1920 play *RUR* – though he maintained that it was actually coined by his brother Josef. The science of *robotics* was imagined by Isaac Asimov long before it became a reality. George Orwell is probably the prophet *par excellence* in this regard, with his *1984* giving us *doublespeak* and *groupthink* as well, of course, as *Big Brother*. And words such as *airlock*, *intergalactic*, *mothership*, *hyperspace*, *humanoid*, *stun gun*, and *genetic engineering* first appeared in the pulp sci-fi of the early twentieth century.

There are also several science-fiction terms that have entered the language without becoming science fact. John Wyndham provided dictionaries with the word *triffid* in his 1951 novel *Day of the Triffids*, and HG Wells' *time machine* has passed into everyday use since its debut in 1895. *Doctor Who* scriptwriter Terry Nation's *Dalek* is iconic both as image and word, as is George Lucas's *jedi*. And the great-grandmother of science fiction has had an especially enduring impact. Mary Shelley bequeathed *Frankenstein* to the language when she introduced his monster to the world in her 1818 novel, and her linguistic legacy lives on through such hybrids as *frankenfood* and **Frankendoodle.**

f-bomb *n.* **drop an f-bomb** to use the word *fuck* in a situation where this might cause great offence [an allusion to the explosive impact of a bomb]

> Not only are we denied the malicious pleasure of Ramsay venting his spleen on a cast of attention-hogging camera whores but the Fox show takes a pair of rusty shears to his vocal chords. In the same way that airplay requirements mean that many hip-hop records end up censored to the degree that they're instrumentals with occasional grunts, Fox deletes Ramsay's every expletive. Worse, he visibly makes the effort to emit a 'bloody' where he'd instinctively drop an f-bomb (*The Guardian*)

fishapod *n. informal* a name for *Tiktaalik roseae,* an extinct species discovered in fossil form in 2006 that is believed to be the missing link between water and land animals [a blend of FISH and (TETR)APOD]. *See* **Mix and match, page 59**

> And, most surprising of all, its pectoral fins included bones that look like nothing less than a primitive wrist and fingers. In short, fishapod adds one more brick, and an especially important one, to the edifice of Darwinian evolution (*Time Magazine*)

flab jab *n. informal* a cosmetic treatment consisting of an injection of chemicals designed to break down fat deposits

She looked like a little girl who had skinned her knees. But there could be a rather more grown-up reason for Nicole Kidman's matching bandages. This week there was speculation that the Aussie actor has become the latest celebrity to have the so-called 'flab jab', used by otherwise slim stars to shift stubborn fat immune to diet and exercise (*The Sun*)

flashpacker *n. informal* an adventurous traveller whose budget stretches beyond the simple hostels and campsites typically used by young backpackers [from FLASH (ostentatious) + (BACK)PACKER]

Enter the Flashpackers. They've got the adventurous outlook of the traditional budget traveller, with one important difference: dosh. Usually in their thirties and forties, Flashpackers are typically on extended holidays, sabbaticals or career breaks. They probably went backpacking in their youth and they've lost none of that gung-ho attitude. It's just that, now, they are equally at home living the simple life in a £3 beach hut or the high life in a five-star hotel (*The Times*)

flexitarian *n.* **1** a person who eats a predominantly vegetarian diet, but who eats meat or fish occasionally | *adj.* **2** of or relating to a flexitarian, eg *flexitarian fare* > **flexitarianism** *n.* [from FLEXI(BLE) + (VEGE)TARIAN]

One type that seems to be proliferating is the 'flexitarian': those who choose to loosen the rules of true vegetarianism by mixing and matching, eating vegetarian food one day, while enjoying anything from oven-baked sea bass to a 6oz steak the next. If you are, or have been, a vegetarian purely for health reasons, flexitarianism could prove to be a win-win way of life (*The Times*)

flog *n.* *informal* a blog that does not reflect the views of a real person, generally used for marketing purposes [F(AKE) + (B)LOG, plus pun on 'flog', 'to sell']

Derided by bloggers, fake blogs are an increasing trend. McDonald's created a flog to accompany its Super Bowl ad about the mock discovery of a French fry shaped like Lincoln, while Captain Morgan created a fake blog in March for its Rum drinks (*Business Week*)

folktronica *n.* *informal* a musical genre that combines elements from folk and electronic music

folk – songs that tap into the traditional roots of the nation's music – is enjoying a renaissance at the moment, with Lou Rhodes of drum'n'bass outfit Lamb pioneering a genre dubbed 'folktronica' (*The Guardian*)

framily *n.* *informal* a close-knit social group that comprises both friends and family members [from FRIEND + FAMILY]

'Friends are the family we choose for ourselves,' said writer Edna Buchanan. But it seems that Britons have gone one better and combined the two, inventing a

new social group – the 'framily'… Research revealed
last week shows that, though one in four of us spend
more time with friends than relatives, 67 per cent of
us consider our best friend to be a member of the
family (*The Observer*)

Frankendoodle *n. informal* a disparaging term for
any purposely cross-bred dog, such as a labradoodle or
a puggle [a blend of FRANKENSTEIN and
LABRADOODLE]

Then are the ethical concerns based around genetic
meddling, which in some cases produce animals
unusually vulnerable to disease. Critics already have a
word for them: they are known as 'Frankendoodles'
(*The Sunday Times*)

frazz *vb. intr informal* to attempt to work quickly on
several different tasks simultaneously, with the result
that none is performed efficiently or to an adequate
standard [a phonetic blend of FRANTIC + MULTITASK,
possibly influenced by FRAZZLED or SPAZZING. Coined
by US psychiatrist Edward Hallowell]

[We spoke to] a marketing consultant in New York
who knows all about multitasking. 'I would say
simultaneously I would have three things going at
once,' he said. 'I'm on the phone, I'm instant
messaging, and reading and responding to e-mails,' he
said. But he says he has no choice; if he's not frazzing,

he might miss something important (*ABC News*)

freakonomics *pl n.* *informal* the application of economic principles to data relating to areas of life outside the normal realm of economics, such as crime rates and sporting results [From the book *Freakonomics* (2005) by Steven Levitt and Stephen J Dubner] > **freakonomic** *adj.*

> This panoply of freakonomic experimentation practically begs the question: Is traditional economic theory all flushed out? Must today's economists resort to dubious offshoots of the discipline in order to establish themselves (*Yale Economic Review*)

freecycle *n.* **1** an informal network of citizens who cooperate online to promote recycling by offering one another unwanted items free of charge | *vb.* *tr* **2** to recycle (an unwanted item) by offering it to someone free of charge

> …getting in at freecycling's grassroots is a great way to reduce the tonnes of junk sent to landfill sites, but there are limits. The North Carolina-based *News & Observer* said some groups have banned live animals, and a potential sperm donor had also been turned down. The organiser of the local Freecycle group commented: 'This was not the appropriate place' (*The Guardian*)

Mix and match

One of the latest creatures to have slithered from the primeval swamp of palaeontology is *Tiktaalik roseae,* a link between fish and land animals recently discovered in the Nunavut Territory of Arctic Canada. **Tiktaalik** has been dead for a mere 383 million years, but its name, Inuktitut in origin, looks set to enter the *Collins English Dictionary* in the near future.

It's nice to see another Inuktitut word enter the English language, joining *anorak, igloo,* and *kayak.* But Tiktaalik's nickname is just as interesting. **Fishapod** not only succinctly encapsulates the nature of this 'fish with feet' (an important missing link between water and land animals), but also highlights an interesting trend in language – the increasing freedom with which we create new hybrids from existing words, regardless of linguistic convention.

Purists will doubtless sneer at the way in which Germanic and Greek words have been spliced together in *fishapod* ('Surely it should be *icthyopod?*'), but these people are probably still bemoaning that egregious Greek-Latin hybrid *television.*

As coinages like **flexitarian, fauxmosexual,** and **tanorexic** show, we are adept at making new words from old, based on punning, allusion, and common sense rather than deference to ancient linguistic principles. These words are memorable, amusing, and – most importantly – easily understood. So the fishapod, our new friend from the distant past, serves as a reminder that English is ours to do with what we will, rather than a fossilized museum exhibit.

freedom bag *n.* a transparent rucksack designed to free the bearer from suspicion of being a suicide bomber [Possibly influenced by *freedom fries,* insofar as 'freedom' seems to be the modifier of choice when setting out opposition to global terrorism]

> And what about the Freedom Bag carriers themselves? By all means, be a good egg and reduce terror for everyone else – but simultaneously increase terror for yourself. Try a few journeys with your iPod, camera phone and wallet displayed in full, clear, durable plastic and just feel that suspicion, paranoia and tension rise. In you (*Londonist.com*)

freemium *adj.* denoting a business practice in which basic services are offered free to customers while more advanced services must be paid for [a blend of FREE and (PRE)MIUM]

> The company makes money by charging users for connecting to phone systems outside of its network. It's a freemium model: Attract users with free services, then charge them a premium for special features (*Wired*)

freeper *n. chiefly US and Canadian, informal* an active member of the Free Republic website, an American right-wing news and discussion forum [from a contraction of FREE + REP(UBLIC)]

> In the first 48 hours after the column [proposing that
> US states who voted Democrat should become part of
> Canada] ran, insulting e-mails from right-wing, web-
> based responders known on-line as freepers
> accumulated like spam in my inbox (*The Globe and
> Mail*)

frenemy *n.* a friend who exhibits hostility to another
[a blend of FR(IEND) and ENEMY; first used in the HBO
TV series *Sex and the City*]

> If you live in a Carrie Bradshaw world then the
> 'frenemies' idea should not be a new one. 'Frenemies'
> are people with whom you have a friendship with but
> neither of you are particularly friendly to each other.
> These types of friends destroy each other's self-
> esteem; they compete desperately with each other and
> see them as competitors. They strive to be better than
> the other in particular aspects of life and often put the
> other down to make them feel like they are winning
> (*friends.teenfx.com*)

friction party *n.* *informal* a social event at which
people touch and rub each other for sexual
gratification, without full sexual intercourse

> The rules at a friction party indicate that there is no
> sex but a lot of touching and rubbing. Couples get
> worked up and go back to their own rooms (*CBS.com
> (programme guide)*)

frigmarole *n. informal* a jocular term for foreplay when considered, esp from the man's point of view, to be a tiresome prelude to the main event [from a blend of FRIG and RIGMAROLE]

> Frigmarole = Aussie for foreplay. It is widely accepted that the New Aussie will have the common courtesy to shout 'Brace yourself, Sheila' before attempting congress (*wossname.thingy.com*)

frost *vb. British* to steal a car whose engine has been left running while the owner de-ices the windscreen > **frosting** *n.*

> Another warning was issued by insurers against 'frosting'... A spokesperson for Sainsbury's bank said 27,000 cars a year over the past five years had been 'frosted' (*The Guardian*)

function creep *n.* the gradual widening of the use of a technology or system beyond the purpose for which it was originally intended, esp when this leads to potential invasion of privacy

> A number of forum participants say with the proper safeguards, people shouldn't fear ID card databases will be abused, but privacy experts have used the notion of what's called 'function creep' as an argument against the ID card. Stephanie Parent, a Montreal privacy consultant, said: 'one of the

arguments is that IBM, by building the systems for Hitler before the war, created census and registration systems that facilitated the rounding up of the Jews' (*CBC News*)

Galactico *n. informal* a famous and highly paid footballer [from Spanish *Los Galacticos* the nickname of the expensively assembled Real Madrid team of the early 21st century; *galactico* someone from another galaxy, denoting their superstar status]

> Chelsea will not be signing David Beckham if you believe the words of boss Jose Mourinho. He slammed the Galacticos, saying: What the devil is a Galactico anyway? Is it a player with a lot of prestige? Or one who can produce a great performance in 60 matches? The image of the Galatico comes from the social lives, publicity and fame that the players have achieved and it is those Galacticos that I distrust (*Megastar Magazine*)

gaymer *n. informal* a gay player of computer games [from GAY + (GA)MER]

> Many pointed out that Warcraft has a thriving community of gay players, or gaymers, and that it made no sense to censor talk about players' sexuality outside [the virtual world of] Azeroth (*BBC Online*)

gee-gee *n. informal* a scientists' nickname for a

global geophysical event, such as a tsunami or an asteroid colliding with Earth [from the initial 'g's of GLOBAL and GEOPHYSICAL]

> The easy option is to lie back and relax, knowing that statistically, we probably won't be around when the next gee-gee strikes (*The Guardian*)

geeksta *n. music US, informal* a style of rap music, characterized by lyrics about computer programming and academic study [modelled on GANGSTA RAP]. *See also* **nerdcore**

> While gangsta rap is seen as celebrating the violence and aggression that claimed two of its brightest stars, 'geeksta' rap is a hip-hop genre celebrating coding skills and school grades (*Wired*)

gemmelsmerch *n.* the power of a given object, person, event, etc, to distract one from one's purpose [Coined by US psychiatrist Edward Hallowell]

> You're a victim of gemmelsmerch when you're distracted from the TV show you are watching by wondering if there's something better on another station (*ProductivityGoal.com*)

Generation C *n. informal* a collective term for the growing number of people who are comfortable creating content for public consumption (esp through the internet), often using sophisticated multimedia tools that were previously the preserve of professionals [C stands for CONTENT]

> However, when Canon tells consumers that its products 'leave one difference between you and a professional. They get paid', they're kind of behind already: talented members of Generation C actually DO get paid, as their stories, their observations, their articles, their pictures, their songs, and their books are noticed and bought by niche audiences (*Trendwatching.com*)

generica *n.* a collective term for those elements of Western culture that are found in similar or identical form all over the world, such as fast-food restaurants, shopping malls, etc, and which, it is suggested, are lending the world an increasingly uniform appearance [from GENERIC + -A, suffix forming plural nouns, and influenced by AMERICA, seen by many as the main driver of globalization. The capitalized form has been trademarked by the creators of a website of the same name that encourages diversity]

> The Grammys are such a snore, such a bore. America loves its generica, as you may have noticed by our 'freedom fries' (go ahead, laugh), our samey retail

chains, assembly-line R&B divas, and bad politicians. It partly translates to our music: the emotionally detached Norah Jones is a completely harmless example of the homogeneity of pop, while punk girl Avril Lavigne isn't quite so genuine as the tweens would have you believe (*The Times*)

geocaching *n.* a game in which the object is to identify and find items deposited by other players, using GPS navigation [from GEO(GRAPHY) + CACHE]

Mary Lee Gunn, 58, a middle-school math teacher from Auburn, N. Y., filled a small black box with marbles last week and carefully hid it along the edge of a canal. Then, when she got home, she posted the box's location along with some digital pictures taken near the spot and hints on how to find it on the Web and invited anybody who was interested to try to find it. If it surprises you that anyone would care enough to take Gunn up on her challenge, then you've probably never heard of geocaching, a high-tech treasure hunt played with handheld versions of the same GPS receivers that have guided missiles with such success in the war in Iraq (*Time Magazine*)

geosequestration *n.* the process of storing carbon dioxide between layers of underground rock in an attempt to reduce (among other things) global warming [from GEO- indicating earth + (CARBON) SEQUESTRATION]

> Victoria is the frontrunner to host Australia's first trial facility in a controversial plan to store carbon dioxide emissions deep underground. Australia, with the US, is championing 'geosequestration' as a means of reducing greenhouse gas emissions – thereby making the world's reliance on fossil fuels, such as coal, oil and gas, environmentally sustainable (*The Australian*)

ghost prisoner *n. informal* a prisoner, esp one held in US military captivity, whose detention is not publicly acknowledged

> The CIA violated Army rules by keeping undocumented 'ghost prisoners' at the prison in Baghdad. At least one of the ghost prisoners died in custody after he was hit in the head with a rifle butt by a Navy SEAL during his capture (*The Washington Times*)

Giganto *n. Gigantopithecus blacki,* an extremely large prehistoric ape [a contraction of GIGANTOPITHECUS, influenced by *Giganto,* an opponent of the Fantastic Four in Marvel Comics]. *See* **Old names for new, page 83**

> Giganto remains are so rare that authorities have never allowed direct dating techniques to be carried out on them, for fear that the process could destroy

bone samples. But by analysing the teeth of other mammal species found in the same layers of soil as the giant ape, including Stegodon, an elephant ancestor, Professor Rink was able to determine that the primate was still living 100,000 years ago (*The Times*)

gling *or* **gling-gling** *n. informal* a collective term for accessories and other items of paraphernalia associated with computers (key drives, swipe cards, promotional mouse mats, etc) [from G(EEK) + (B)LING]

> Wow, I'm really impressed with this new generation of security for our gling-gling ... I really like the screen lock (*Mobility Today forum*)

global dimming *n.* a decrease in the amount of sunlight reaching the surface of the earth, believed to be caused by pollution in the atmosphere

> Recently, however, this brown haze was deemed harmful to...oh I don't know, babies and old people, I should think ... so the world's governments decided it should be removed. As a result, power stations were forced to fit scrubbers and cars were fitted with catalytic converters. And now, the haze is going away. Hurrah, you might think. But no. It seems the soot and particulates have been blocking out the sunlight causing what they're calling global dimming. And this has been masking the true extent of global warming (*The Sun*)

Open-source English

In the language of software developers, English has gone open-source. Like computer codes that are made freely available to anyone who wants to use them, the English language is being adopted and adapted in myriad different forms around the world. The narrow divide between British and American English now represents only a small part of an increasingly complex picture. Not only are there distinct types of English in Anglophone countries, there are also English-based modes of speech and writing in places where it is a second language. *Hinglish, Japlish, Singlish, Konglish,* and *Chinglish* exemplify this trend of English merging with the speech patterns and vocabulary of non-native speakers.

Another development is the growth of simplified lexicons such as **Globish** and **globespeak** that use English as a template. Proponents of these argue that what many people use for communication is no longer English, but new languages derived from it.

Meanwhile, the internet is creating online communities with private languages, based on – but removed from – Standard English, as with **Leetspeak. Leet,** or **1337** as it is often represented, is an exclusive form of English spelling designed to enhance the 'elite' status of its users.

Standard English can now be considered just one dialect among many. Rather than speaking of a single language, we might do better to talk about different 'Englishes' in different parts of the world, and in different communities, whether actual or 'virtual'.

globesity *n.* *informal* obesity seen as a worldwide social problem [from GL(OBAL) + OBESITY]

> … the obesity epidemic in America has burst the zipper of geography and is spreading all over the world in a phenomenon dubbed 'globesity'. For the first time, the numbers of overweight and underfed people are balanced at 1.1 billion (*The Herald*)

globespeak *n.* a type of English, common in electronic forms of communication such as email and text messaging, in which familiar British expressions are replaced by short informal words often derived from US or Australian English [from GLOBE + -SPEAK]

> Traditional greetings like 'hello' are being replaced by the language of e-mail and text messaging, a new report has found. And the constant use of slang words could see basic words like 'goodbye' made obsolete within a generation. People using new technologies to communicate are much more likely to start the conversation 'hey' and sign it off 'laters' than the more formal alternatives, says the study. The report's authors blamed the rise of 'globespeak' – people from all over the world using the same shorthand. (*BBC Online*)

Globish *n.* a simplified version of English that is used by non-native English speakers and consists of only the most common words and phrases [a blend of

It's been a problem since the days of the Tower of Babel trying to communicate with others when you don't speak a common language. We went to a downtown Vancouver Youth Hostel, to hear from guests and staff about problems caused by the language barrier and ways to overcome them. Well, Jean-Paul Nerriere doesn't have to resort to charades or screaming to communicate with people who don't speak his native French. He has developed what he believes is a unique communications tool that he calls Globish. And it's capturing the attention of people and companies around the world who've had mini 'Tower of Babble' troubles. (*Canadian Broadcasting Corporation*)

Godcast *n.* a religious service or sermon that has been converted to MP3 format for download from the internet for play on a computer or MP3 player [GOD + POD(CAST)]

Lee Rainie, director of the Pew Internet and American Life Project, told the Washington Post that 'Godcasting' means 'you can get your dose of your worship service when you want it, not necessarily when it's taking place' (*The Times*)

Godzilla *n.* *informal* an extinct marine reptile, *Dakosaurus andiniensis,* of the Cretaceous period, having jagged teeth and a snout like that of a tyrannosaur [After the Japanese film monster, itself originally *Gojira*, a portmanteau word suggesting 'Gorilla-whale']. *See* **Old names for new, page 83**

> Scientists have nicknamed it Godzilla, but it really belongs in another movie, one not yet made but possibly titled: 'Jaws Meets Jurassic Park' (*The New York Times*)

gogan *n. Australian, informal, derogatory* a young person who combines trends of goth fashion with dress and behaviour identified with uncouth, white, working-class stereotypes; such people are perceived as not being 'true' goths. *Also called* **bogoths** [from G(OTH) + (B)OGAN the derogatory Australian term for a stereotypically uncouth, white, working-class person]

> Oh man, it was so fucking hilarious yesterday. The goths and gogans were sitting in Forrest Chase, and some punks walked past, and the goths and punks started having an argument, each saying that the other group were so lame (*perthbands.com forum*)

googlearchy *n. internet, informal* the ranking of websites by search engines according to popularity [from the search engine Google a trademark + (HIER)ARCHY]

> The winner takes all, it is widely supposed in

computing circles. Indeed, geeks have coined a word, 'Googlearchy', for the way in which search engines encourage web traffic towards the most popular sites (*The Economist*)

google bombing *n. informal* the practice of attempting to affect the ranking of websites provided by the Google *trademark* search engine

> Google-bombing has fast become a popular prank on the Web. Bloggers have found they can manipulate search results by hyperlinking unsavory labels to individual pages. The trick also works on Yahoo, Lycos and altavista... Bush has been bombed as well. The search 'miserable failure' now brings up his official White House biography. He also was bombed last year with the phrase 'dumb motherfucker' (*Wired*)

Googlejuice *n. internet, informal* **a** the supposedly mysterious quality that enables a website to attain a high ranking on search engines, esp on Google *trademark* **b** the power or influence that comes with having a high ranking on search engines [from Google a trademark + JUICE (in slang sense meaning 'power, influence, etc')]

> Having achieved such a rank he could then profit from the Googlejuice by selling outbound links from the site (*Wired*)

Great Firewall *or* **Great Firewall of China** *n.* a system
that prevents access to internet sites deemed
undesirable by the government of the People's
Republic of China [a play on the Great Wall of China;
a FIREWALL is a computer system that prevents
unauthorized access to the internet]

> Google has claimed that Chinese surfers can use its
> main portal, Google.com, to read material that does
> not appear on the censored site. But it is thought that
> Mr Brin's comments may have been precipitated by
> reports that the international site has been
> inaccessible throughout much of China for long
> periods of time – apparently blocked by the so-called
> Great Firewall, which prevents access to websites the
> government deems unsavoury (*The Guardian*)

green footprint *n.* the impact of a building on the
environment

> In Germany, more than 100 million sq m of green
> roof have been created; in many regions planning
> consent is given only when the 'green footprint' of the
> building is replicated on the roof (*The Times*)

green-light district *n.* an area in which prostitution is
officially tolerated [from GREEN LIGHT, modelled on
RED-LIGHT DISTRICT]

> Britons spend more on the sex industry than on

cinema tickets. Now the law is set for a shake-up, with
a possibility that 'green-light districts' where selling
sex is tolerated could be introduced (*BBC News*)

griefer *or* **grief player** *n.* an online game player who
intentionally spoils the game for other players

> [Mr X] and his wife, Jennifer, are two of the more
> hard-core Sims™ players. They log several hours
> most days. After the Las Vegas couple distributed
> photos of themselves to friends, one griefer hacked
> into [Mr X]'s America Online account and stole his in-
> game character's possessions. Someone else posed as
> [Mr X] and told other players that Jennifer had died of
> cancer (*The Globe and Mail*)

grime *n.* a genre of music originating in the East End
of London and combining elements of garage, hip-
hop, rap, and jungle [of uncertain origin]

> Grime vocalists resemble turbo-charged rappers,
> racing to match backing tracks that thump about 130
> times per minute – near your target heart rate for
> vigorous physical activity (*CBC News*)

grup *n.* *informal* a person aged over thirty who has
similar interests and lifestyle to those of people in
their early twenties [a contraction of GROWN-UP
influenced by a 1966 episode of *Star Trek* in which the
protagonists land on a planet ruled by children who

refer to adults as 'grups']. *See* **Who are you, page 109**

> If being a Grup means being 35, and having a job, and
> using a messenger bag instead of a briefcase, and
> staying out too late too often, and owning more pairs
> of sneakers (eleven) than suits (one), and downloading
> a Hot Hot Heat song from iTunes™ because it was on
> a playlist titled 'Saturday Errands,' and generally being
> uneasy and slightly confused about just what it means
> to be an adult in these modern times – in short, if it
> means living your life in fundamentally the same way
> that you did when you were, say, 22 – then, let's face it,
> I'm a Grup (*New York magazine*)

guerrilla store *n.* a designer fashion shop that opens
for a limited period, typically situated in an unusual or
downmarket location and advertised through an
unconventional marketing campaign. *Also called* **pop-
up shop**

> Avant-garde Japanese designers Commes des
> Garcons opened a 'guerrilla store' – with no phone
> listing, no signage – in a Berlin backstreet, with plans
> to close down after 12 months even if the shop made a
> profit. They've since opened other guerrilla stores in
> Barcelona, Singapore and, for one month only, in
> Tokyo (*The Age*)

guerrilla gig *n.* an impromptu musical performance
in an unlikely public space, such as an underground
train or on the roof of a building, organised by text-

message communication between the band and its fans

> Dom Masters – The Others (after storming Radio 1 HQ): 'The BBC wanted to do an interview with me about guerrilla gigging – so we thought we'd bring you a guerrilla gig. I thought you'd like it. Your security didn't feel the same way, but they were pretty amicable with us, they let us do four songs. We had two pig-amps, a child's drum kit and I used one of them megaphones!' (*BBC Radio 1*)

hangover hospital *n. informal* a clinic for the care of patients who have drunk too much alcohol or who have suffered alcohol-related injuries, held in an area popular with drinkers and during a period (eg a weekend) in which a high volume of alcohol is expected to be drunk

> Makeshift field clinics should be set up in cities across Britain to deal with minor alcohol-related injuries, according to those behind the UK's first all-night 'hangover hospital', which opened in Newcastle this weekend (*The Observer*)

happy slapping *n. British, informal* the crime of attacking, often slapping, an unsuspecting passer-by and filming it with a mobile camera phone, footage of which is then circulated for the amusement of others

A 16-year-old girl arrested after an attack on a teenager that was filmed on a mobile video phone has been bailed by police until next month. The 16-year-old victim was knocked out and suffered temporary paralysis when she was attacked near her Manchester home. The teenager from Blackley, who went into a police station voluntarily, was questioned on suspicion of assault, a police spokeswoman said. The attack was filmed on a mobile phone – a craze known as 'happy slapping' (*BBC Online*)

Helengrad *n. New Zealand, informal* a nickname for Wellington, New Zealand, satirizing the alleged political correctness and socialist leanings of the government led by Helen Clark [from *Helen* (Clark), NZ Prime Minister since 1999 + -GRAD, common combining form in the names of Russian cities]

But the second-term drift and mistakes have crumbled Helengrad's ramparts. If Clark is to command votes in 2008 she needs now to command policy – to be proactive, not just reactive (*The New Zealand Herald*)

heteroflexible *adj.* **1** (of a person) predominantly heterosexual but not exclusively so | *n.* **2** such a person [from HETERO(SEXUAL) + FLEXIBLE]

They lead dangerous lives; they ingest dangerous substances such as fried dog or spray-on macrobiotic enzymes; they mostly live in morally-questionable cities such as Budapest or San Francisco. The late-developers are fond of Trappist and yogic retreats, and they are either heteroflexible, or having an affair with a difficult Russian with gold nail varnish (*The Times*)

heteropolitan *n. informal* a man who achieves a balance between old and new ideals of manliness, with an interest both in grooming and in traditional masculine pursuits [HETERO(SEXUAL) + (METRO)POLITAN; an inversion of METROSEXUAL]

Neither lager-loving sexists obsessed with football nor excessively moisturised, pink-shirted effeminates, Heteropolitans enjoy both the pub and the grooming parlour, and are surprisingly committed to relationships and family life (*The Guardian*)

hikikomori *n.* **1** a Japanese social phenomenon in which people (usually young men) withdraw from society, often confining themselves to a single room and engaging only in such interaction with others as is necessary to stay alive **2** a person who withdraws in such a manner [from Japanese: a withdrawal]

Like anorexia, which has been largely limited to Western cultures, hikikomori is a culture-bound syndrome that thrives in one particular country during a particular moment in its history. For all the attention, though, hikikomori remains confounding. The Japanese public has blamed everything from smothering mothers to absent, overworked fathers, from school bullying to the lacklustre economy, from academic pressure to video games (*The New York Times*)

hillbilly armour *n. US, military, informal* makeshift armour consisting of scavenged steel welded onto military vehicles, especially prevalent in Iraq [in allusion to the supposed hillbilly characteristic of reclaiming discarded machinery, etc]

They call it 'hillbilly armor' – US military vehicles protected with scrap metal salvaged from landfills. And now US soldiers want to know how long they will have to scavenge for junk to protect themselves in combat (*ABC News*)

hobbit *n.* a nickname adopted for a very small type of primitive human, *Homo floresiensis,* following the discovery of remains of eight such people on the Island of Flores, Indonesia, in 2004 [HOBBIT was originally coined by British writer J. R. R. Tolkien (1892–1973) to describe an imaginary race of diminutive human-like beings in his novels *The Hobbit* and *The Lord of the Rings*]

Dr Brown loathes having his tiny proto-human being called the Hobbit. If anybody uses the word, he puts the phone down. But if anything is certain in this world, it is that the name will stick (*The Times*)

homeshoring *n.* the practice among employers of paying employees to work from home rather than an office. *Also called* **homesourcing** [blend of HOME + (OFF)SHORING]

The next customer service agent you get on the phone may well be sitting in slippers and a bathrobe. A report released Tuesday from research firm IDC says a number of companies are turning to a new method to meet call center challenges: getting workers to handle calls from their homes. So-called homeshoring or homesourcing in certain situations can boost productivity while cutting costs, according to researcher IDC. The practice also can avoid a potential pitfall of sending such work overseas, IDC suggested: foreign agents less familiar with US customers (*news.com.com*)

hose rage *n. Australian, informal* anger and confrontation caused by disputes over water restrictions

The tranquility of Australia's suburbs is under threat from 'hose rage', the confrontational and occasionally violent fallout of strict water restrictions introduced after a prolonged drought. The restrictions, which

include a ban on sprinklers, have resulted in
neighbours exchanging blows and the authorities
receiving thousands of tip-offs about people flouting
the rules *(The Independent)*

hyote *n. US, informal* a name given to an animal
sighted frequently in Maryland, USA in 2004 and taken
to be a cross between a hyena and a coyote. It was
eventually identified as a red fox suffering from a skin
disease which had caused it to lose most of its hair,
leaving a mane on the neck and shoulders like that of a
hyena [from HY(ENA) + (COY)OTE]

> The beast is not shy, and visits most often under
> bright sun. While no one here knows what it is, they
> do have a name for it – the hyote, a combination of a
> hyena and a coyote *(NBC13.com)*

ICE *abbreviation for* in case of emergency: listed as a
contact in a person's mobile phone and meant to be
the first number to be called by emergency services if
that person is involved in an accident

> East Anglian Ambulance Service have launched a
> national 'In case of Emergency (ICE)' campaign … The
> idea is that you store the word 'ICE' in your mobile
> phone address book, and against it enter the number
> of the person you would want to be contacted 'In Case
> of Emergency' *(The Register)*

Old names for new

Hobbits have been making the headlines in the twenty-first century, and not only through Peter Jackson's *Lord of the Rings* movies. The discovery of tiny skeletons on the Indonesian island of Flores has given the half-sized humans another lease of life.

The word *hobbit* was coined by JRR Tolkien in the 1920s. Tolkien 'derived' the word from *holbylta,* which would have been the Anglo-Saxon for 'hole-dweller'. Tolkien's little people have entered the popular consciousness along with a bestiary of comic-book, cinematic, and literary creations, forming a kind of modern mythology. And so it's no surprise that terms from this popular mythology are being used where names from 'proper' mythology were previously employed – in naming the weird and wonderful creatures of the real word.

So, just as we have the *basilisk* (an Australian lizard), the *chimaera* (a deep-sea fish), and the *hydra* (a freshwater polyp), as well as *harpy* eagles, *griffon* vultures, *goblin* sharks, *salamanders*, *pythons* and, of course, the Komodo *dragon*, we now have the **hobbit** (*Homo floresiensis*), **Godzilla** (*Dakosaurus andiniensis*), and **Giganto** (*Gigantopithecus blacki*).

These creatures from the distant past are as bizarre and exotic as anything from the realms of fantasy fiction, and so the nicknames they take from pop-culture are perfectly apt. As palaeontologists unearth more of our monstrous antecedents, we can expect to see the terminology of comic books and sword and sorcery reused with increasing frequency.

hyote
Old names for new

infomania *n. informal* an obsession with keeping up to date with one's emails, text messages, etc [a blend of INFORMATION and MANIA]

> Workers distracted by email and phone calls suffer a fall in IQ more than twice that found in marijuana smokers, new research has claimed. The study for computing firm Hewlett Packard warned of a rise in 'infomania', with people becoming addicted to email and text messages. Researchers found 62% of people checked work messages at home or on holiday. The firm said new technology can help productivity, but users must learn to switch computers and phones off (*BBC Online*)

in silico *adj.* **1** (of biological processes) imitated by computer simulation and mathematical modelling | *adv.* **2** by this method [New Latin, literally: in silicon]

> The most complex object known to humanity is the human brain – and not only is it complex, but it is the seat of one of the few natural phenomena that science has no purchase on at all, namely consciousness. To try to replicate something that is so poorly understood may therefore seem like hubris. But you have to start somewhere, and IBM and the Ecole Polytechnique Fédérale de Lausanne (EPFL), in Switzerland, propose to start by replicating 'in silico', as the jargon has it, one of the brain's building blocks (*The Economist*)

internet pure play *or* **pure internet play** *n.* a company that trades solely on the internet

> Offline retailers, once considered dinosaurs by so-called internet pure plays, are threatening to overwhelm online-only retailers, according to a report released yesterday (*Direct Magazine*)

inverse graffiti *n.* a form of street art in which a dirty wall or pavement has a template placed against it and is scrubbed until the surface is clean. This reveals an image or message which gradually fades with time

> A British street artist known as Moose creates graffiti by cleaning dirt from sidewalks and tunnels – sometimes for money when the images are used as advertising. But some authorities call it vandalism. Moose … got the idea when he saw that people had written their names with their fingers on dirty tunnel walls in his hometown of Leeds. Moose does some freehand drawing, but also uses the grid from wall tiles to create perfect shapes and letters. The tools are simple: a shoe brush, water and elbow grease, he says (*National Public Radio*)

iPill *n.* a pill containing a microchip that is programmed to release the appropriate dosage of a drug following a diagnosis of the patient's ailment [I(NTELLIGENT) + PILL]

Microchip-loaded, intelligent pills soon could be used to diagnose a patient's condition after being swallowed and compute the best, safest amount of drugs to treat diseases. Their inventors say the iPills, as the devices are called, could become lifesavers in emergency situations, dispensing precise doses of medication even when doctors are unavailable. The iPills also could be programmed to release drugs precisely in complicated schedules, an ability of critical importance for diseases such as cancer or AIDS, where cocktails of many different medications often are required at constant intervals (*smalltimes.com*)

iPorn *n. informal* pornography downloaded for viewing on a video MP3 player [a blend of iPod a trademark + PORN]

Can you even imagine the amazing iPorn ads just around the corner? I can't. It's sheer sensory overload. iPod™ porn is here to stay, and society will unquestionably say iDo (*The Harvard Independent*)

Jack *n. US, informal* **1** a radio format in which a large number of songs are preprogrammed and then played in a random order, often with a recorded voice rather than a live presenter making brief remarks between songs **2** as modifier: *Jack radio* [from 'Cadillac Jack' Garret, an imaginary radio personality invented in 2000 by US DJ Bob Perry, creator of the format]

> Unlike a typical radio station, which regularly plays 300 or 400 hits of a particular genre, programmers on Jack stations select 700 to 1,000 songs of completely different genres. Then, they sequence them to create what radio programmers call 'train wrecks' – Billy Idol will follow Bob Marley, Elvis after Guns N' Roses, and so on (*Business Week*)

Jafaican or **Jafaikan** *n. chiefly British, informal* **1** a London dialect of English with marked Jamaican influences **2** a white person who adopts Jamaican modes of expression [a blend of JAMAICAN and FAKE]

> What has emerged is a distinctive inner-London patois which borrows heavily from Jamaican creole, lifting some words unchanged. An analysis of vowel sounds has shown the traditional long Cockney vowels are becoming shorter. The word 'face' sounds like 'fice' in cockney but more like 'fehs' in Jafaican (*The Daily Mail*)

jet-to-let *adj. chiefly British, informal* relating to the practice of buying a home abroad for rental as an investment: *a jet-to-let investor*

> According to a survey today, this 'jet-to-let' generation is likely to shell out an average of £101,000 for an overseas property, compared with the average cost in

Britain of £160,000 (*The Guardian*)

job-dumping *n.* the practice of giving a job to the person who is willing to do it for the least amount of money. A vacant position is advertised on a website and would-be employees bid against each other, each stating their lowest acceptable wage [from the name of the first website dedicated to this practice]

> A young entrepreneur is enjoying success in Germany after developing a website that allows people to bid for work by undercutting others. He is now in talks to set up so-called 'job-dumping' sites in other countries (*BBC News*)

kakuro *n.* a Japanese logic puzzle, in which a player inserts numbers into a grid resembling that of a crossword [from Japanese *kasan* addition + *kurosu* a transliteration of English CROSS]

> Kakuro is Japan's best-kept secret, a puzzle that millions prefer to sudoku (*The Guardian*)

Kapa o Pango *n. rugby union New Zealand* a variety of All Black haka, which includes a throat-slitting gesture [Maori: 'the black team']

> Saturday's performance of Kapa O Pango was the culmination of more than a year's development, and it

left the Ngati Porou man [haka composer Derek
Lardelli] humbled and proud at the energy and
passion displayed by the team (*The New Zealand
Herald*)

kipper *n. informal* an adult who cannot afford to
move away from the parental home [singular is a back
formation from *k(ids) i(n) p(arents') p(ockets) e(roding)
r(etirement) s(avings)*]

> Adult children who still live at home are now known
> as 'Kippers' – it's an acronym meaning Kids In Parents'
> Pockets Eroding Retirement Savings. Funny, but I
> always thought there was another word for them –
> scroungers (*The Edmonton Sun*)

krumping *n.* a type of dancing in which participants,
often wearing face paint, dance with one another in a
fast and aggressive style mimicking a fight but without
any violence [origin unknown] > **krumper** *n.*
> **krump** *vb.*

> … it has evolved in 'its own subculture among teens
> in such … [LA] neighbourhoods as Compton, South
> Central and Watts,' said the Winston-Salem Journal.
> 'Groups gather in school grounds, parking lots and
> yards to perform and 'battle dance' each other. They
> are typically vocal opponents of violence, thus making
> the scene an alternative to the gang wars that plague
> the areas where krumping is popular' (*The Guardian*)

lactivist *n.* a woman who strongly advocates the breastfeeding of children, esp one who breastfeeds her children long after they are no longer babies [a blend of LACTATE and ACTIVIST]

> So far as I know, babies in Britain do not become dangerously hooked on the bottle. It does seem, however, that some adults are becoming seriously attached to breast-feeding. Like that Atlantic-hopping mother, they believe that children should be breast-fed until they are 2, 3, 4 – even 7. In the United States these women are dubbed 'militant lactivists', fighting for a woman's right to stay home and breast-feed her walking, talking infants (*The Times*)

ladult *n. informal* a responsible and financially solvent man in his late twenties or early thirties who still enjoys many things traditionally associated with young males (gadgets, football, drinking, etc)

> Blokes, we feel for you. You have been rebranded so many times it's no wonder you've got yourselves into a tizzy. There were those sissified metros (so over!) and of course those mummy-loving kidults. And now the latest exhortation to emerge from the buzzword pool has arrived: he's the Ladult – a man that still acts like a boy yet knows when to switch into adult-mode (*The Sydney Morning Herald*)

lamestream *n. informal* **1** the traditional media, as opposed to the **blogosphere 2** as modifier: *the lamestream media* [a blend of LAME and MAINSTREAM]

> The irresponsible reporting habits of today's lamestream press are unconscionable (*Capitol Hill Journal*)

lawfare *n. international relations* the use by a country of the law against its enemies, esp in challenging the legality of their military or foreign policy [a blend of LAW and WARFARE]

> We've finally come around, then, after much talk of 'asymmetric warfare,' to officially defining one type of asymmetric warfare as the use of law for nefarious ends. Better to talk turkey about 'lawfare' – especially in an important document like the NDS, which lays the groundwork for the 2005 Quadrennial Defense Review – than to pretend it doesn't ever happen. It does (*The Washington Times*)

leet *n.* **1.** *Short for* **leetspeak 2** | *adj.* impassioned about and highly skilled in the field of advanced computer programming. *Also represented (in leetspeak) as* **1337** [short for ELITE, as the people who use this language consider themselves to be]

> I give it 6 months before people quit looking up to Google as some really leet organization (*slashdot.org forum comment*)

leetspeak *n.* internet jargon in which standard English is translated into a mixture of letters, numerals, symbols, and other characters found on a computer keyboard. This language is often employed by groups on the internet to maintain exclusivity

> Although both guides have been around for a while, they are nevertheless interesting if you haven't seen them before – whether you find them amusing or perhaps even useful – in the way in which they attempt to demystify things like 'leetspeak', often in the context of online gaming or related activities. Leetspeak is described as 'the digital equivalent of pig Latin with a twist of hieroglyphics', and Microsoft's guide notes that the online language rarely respects the rules of grammar and leaves mistakes uncorrected (*eurogamer.net*)

liability engineering *n.* the practice by a company of taking steps to avoid liability for any fraudulent dealings with it, such as making a credit card owner responsible for any abuses of the card by a third party

> So why are banks and retailers so very eager to shepherd in the new system? Hidden in all the song and dance about chip-and-pin systems is also a project that's 'not so much about risk reduction as liability engineering', argues Ross Anderson, professor of security engineering at Cambridge University … What chip-and-pin allows them to do, according to

Anderson, is claim a kind of pre-emptive carte blanche. They can start by imputing negligence – 'You naughty person, you've been a bit careless with that pin, haven't you? Our new systems are secure, so it must be your fault' (*The Guardian*)

lily-pad base *n.* one of a series of lightly-manned military installations situated around a potential source of conflict [analogy with the pattern formed by water lilies on a pond]

Instead, the new military is to maintain a handful of large transport hubs, such as the Ramstein air base in Germany, through which troops could flow to any of a large number of bare-bones 'lily pad' bases and airfields everywhere from the far corners of Central Asia to the deserts of the Middle East, the steppes of Mongolia and the Horn of Africa (*The Scotsman*)

living bandage *n.* a method of treating severe burns or other skin injuries in which cultured cells grown from a sample of the patient's own skin are applied to the wound in order to stimulate new cell growth and avoid problems of graft rejection

A former prisoner of war, now in his 80s, who developed ulcers on his legs while interned in a Japanese camp, was successfully treated with the 'living bandage' after failing to respond to various treatments over the past 60 years (*The Scotsman*)

Mob rule

While the internet best exemplifies the effect that technology has on our language, the mobile phone is having a considerable impact too. Mobiles are ubiquitous and increasingly multifunctional. It's not the phone function of the mobile that's expanding our vocabulary, but the other applications, from **phonetography** to downloading songs and films to paying bills. The development of the **mobile wallet,** for example, suggests that phones will increasingly be the essential 'all-in-one' gadget involved in a huge range of our daily activities.

In its media-player incarnation, the mobile is a means of entertainment as well as communication. Games, books, films and TV serials can all be downloaded to phones, spawning a new set of mobile-related terms. Thus, *mob-* and *moby-* represent the handset in words like **mobysoaps** and **mobisode.**

Our growing dependence on mobiles is changing our behaviour. The culture of texting, with its associated abbreviations, is one obvious example. Another is **pranking:** calling a friend for one or two rings before ending the call so that they call you back and pay for the conversation. Fixed arrangements have largely given way to **approximeeting.** And the camera function of 3G mobiles gives rise to activities ranging from the dangerously antisocial to the harmlessly bizarre. **Phone chicken** is bad enough, but **mobile bullying** and **happy slapping** have become real menaces. **Stealth disco,** however, shows that camphones can be put to more light-hearted use.

Londonistan *n. informal* London considered as a base for radical Islamists [From LONDON + -*stan* a common combining form meaning 'land' in the names of many predominantly Muslim countries; the 'i' is used to echo PAKISTAN, AFGHANISTAN, etc]

> Any number of foreign terror suspects are currently enjoying the hospitality of the British taxpayer because we refuse to extradite them to friendly countries such as Israel, Yemen and Egypt. Is it any wonder our capital city is known internationally as Londonistan? (*The Sun*)

manscaping *n. informal* the trimming or shaving of a man's body hair for cosmetic reasons

> Soccer star David Beckham may be leading the charge of men who have taken up 'manscaping' – getting rid of unwanted hair (*Canada.com*)

massclusivity *n.* the quality of seeming to be exclusive while actually being available for money to many [from MASS (MARKET) + (EX)CLUSIVITY]

> Private members' clubs such as the Groucho and Soho House are now available to all, with places like Milk and Honey and the Firehouse offering the same deal with no snotty selection procedures. Exclusivity for the masses – or massclusivity, as it's become known. Everyone now demands the right to luxury, and we want it at a reasonable price (*The Times*)

masstige *n.* **1** the impression of prestige or luxury in goods that are affordable for many people | *adj.* **2** (of goods) produced by a luxury brand but intended for the mass market in terms of price and availability [from MASS (MARKET) + PRESTIGE]

> Cruising along, enjoying a sunny day and a nifty open car from France, you soon start thinking that this masstige way of life is pretty good. Masstige? You've never heard of it? Nor had I before Peugeot unveiled its newest offering, the 307cc, a convertible with a folding steel roof instead of the more common canvas lid. Seems that masstige is what this car – petite, in the $50,000 bracket – is all about (*The Courier-Mail*)

meatpuppet *n.* a person who joins an online community at the behest of another person solely to provide support for that person's opinions. *See also* **sockpuppet** [modelled on SOCKPUPPET; in internet communities MEAT is often used to denote the real 'fleshy' world as opposed to the virtual world]
> **meatpuppeteer** *n.* > **meatpuppetry** *n.*

> One realizes after being inside Wikipedia, behind the many so-called facts and figures, that there are networks within a network. Some good, some bad. A few respond with vicious relentless assaults that would make the Mafia proud. They can accuse you of

being a 'sockpuppet' or a user who is accessing several computers using several identities. One can also be accused of being a 'meatpuppet', that is, being the friend of a user. I never really understood what was criminal about having friends in Wikipedia? And if you are merely suspected of being a 'sockpuppet' or 'meatpuppet' you can and will be blocked from editing! (*Israel News Agency*)

me-casting *n. informal* a humorous description of podcasting, emphasizing the egocentric aspects of creating one's own online broadcast

She [Chris Mays, programme director for a Seattle radio station] said terrestrial radio is 'leapfrogging' over satellite radio, taking the medium from 'from broadcasting to me-casting... People would rather pay for things they can create themselves (*FutureOfMusic.org*)

memorial diamond *n.* a diamond created from carbon extracted from the remains of a cremated body

The churchyard increasingly is being bypassed as Britons search for ever more creative farewells for their loved ones... One company in Hove, Sussex, charges £11,000 to extract the carbon from a sample of ashes to create a 'memorial diamond' (*The Times*)

menoporsche *n. informal* the phenomenon of middle-aged men attempting to recapture their lost

youth by buying of an expensive sports car [a blend of
MENOPAUSE and PORSCHE, a German manufacturer of
high-performance sports cars]

> Menopause – it's no longer just for women … Dr
> Harry Fisch, a New York physician and author of the
> 'Male Biological Clock,' drolly refers to the
> phenomenon as 'menoporsche,' noting that
> testosterone treatment may prove a better antidote
> for the condition than the purchase of a new sports
> car (*Sunday Herald*)

microcasting *or* **narrowcasting** *n.* the creation of
downloadable audio files aimed at a specialist interest
group rather than a general audience [MICRO- +
(POD)CASTING]

> One aspect of this renaissance is 'narrowcasting' or
> 'microcasting' – broadcasts targeted at niche
> audiences. It is radio that focuses on particular
> interest groups. Examples include 'The Mommycast: a
> podcast for mommies everywhere', or 'The Good Beer
> Show', which offers reviews of micro-brewed beer
> hosted from a tavern in Indiana (*BBC Online*)

microgeneration *n.* the local generation of electrical
power, through means such as wind power or solar
power

> The advocates of the microgeneration revolution are
> keen to encourage us to produce locally, to the point

of producing personally. Or not producing at all. As a recent editorial in the *Independent* put it, 'small actions such as putting on an extra sweater instead of turning up the heating … will help the planet' (*spiked-online.com*)

micro-grom *n. Australian, informal* **1** a junior surfer, esp one under the age of 10 **2** a board of a suitable size for such a surfer [from GROMMET a young surfer]

> 'I told them just to enjoy themselves,' says Wayne of the advice he gave to [his sons] Jimmi and Noah. 'They're having fun and it's not too serious. This event is not a bad idea but I wouldn't like to see too many of them because surfing should be more about fun at that age. Give them a taste but not too much.' Wayne says Noah's lead-up to the micro-grom comp has been been interrupted by an injury and he is likely to be out of the surf until the start of the contest tomorrow (*The Courier-Mail*)

micro-multinational *n.* a small company, usually in the information technology sector, that outsources work to freelancers and other companies abroad

> Yogen Dalal, a partner at Mayfield, says more than half the companies he funds have offshore workers. The Valley even has a name for these startups: micro-multinationals (*Wired*)

micronation *n.* an entity that seeks or purports to

seek sovereign status as an independent nation, but which is unrecognized by real nations, and whose physical borders, if there are any (some exist only in theory or on the internet), extend no further than the private property of its members [from MICRO- + NATION]

> Danny Wallace claims the title of King of the micronation situated in East London, but citizens of Lovely (who become citizens through entering their details on the micronation's website or its section of the BBC website) are invited to declare a room in their own house (or indeed the entire house itself) to be an embassy for the country, by taking a photograph displaying Lovely's flag within their dwelling (*Omnipelagos.com*)

milblog *n.* a web log written by a member of the military, usually someone with a low rank, while on active service [a blend of MILITARY and BLOG]
> **milblogger** *n.*

> There was a time when soldiers' tales of war were recounted in censored letters or heavy tomes written years after the conflict (James Hider in Baghdad writes). But in army tents across Iraq, soldiers sit down every day at computers and put their first-hand accounts straight onto the internet, sometimes just hours after a battle. Milblogs – the online jargon for military weblogs – have become a phenomenon of

modern warfare (*The Times*)

milf *n. slang* a sexually attractive middle-aged woman [from *m(other) i('d) l(ike to) f(uck)*]

> With the exception of one gangsta-styled submission in which attractive, young naked women made out on a motorcycle, the median age of the people on the screen appeared to be 45. Milfs might be a guilty pleasure in pop culture, but this wasn't any 12-year-old's wet dream. Near the end of the film, when a saggy-skinned, frizzy-gray-haired happy-go-lucky woman straddled a horse with her breasts exposed, someone cried out, 'Noooooooh, Grandma!' (*The Phoenix*)

Mini-Man *n. informal* a nickname for the recently discovered *Homo floresiensis*. *See* **hobbit**

> The arrival of 'Mini-Man' is going to give them [Fundamentalist Christians who refute Darwin] nightmares. How can he be 'semi-special'? That won't make sense. He can't very well have a semi-soul. So Mini-Man might just be the evolutionary jewel that, once and for all, sets human beings firmly in the animal kingdom, where scientifically they belong (*Desmond Morris speaking on BBC Online*)

misery memoir *n.* a published memoir that details an unhappy period in the writer's life, such as childhood neglect or abuse

From Dave Pelzer to the latest women's magazine, the misery memoir is a surefire bestseller. But why are we so addicted to other people's agony? (*The Observer*)

moantone *n.* a mobile-phone ringtone that consists of sexually suggestive moaning

Ringtones are yesterday's news. The truly cutting edge (and unflappable) will be signing up for 'moantones'. Porn queen Jenna Jameson is teaming with Wicked Wireless to provide music, R-rated wallpaper and her own brand of ringtones to cell phone subscribers in Latin America. 'Everyone needs a moantone,' Jameson said in a press release (*networkworld.com*)

mobcasting *n.* the use of mobile telephony to create or disseminate audio or video files which can be downloaded from the internet [from MOBILE + (BROAD)CASTING; modelled on PODCASTING]

All we need now is empower people with video phones, 3G mobile telephony, and a Flickr-like tool to upload audio and video to RSS-enabled websites. This is not mobile blogging or podcasting now – we're talking about a social revolution and that's mobcasting (*Google Groups*)

mobile bullying *n.* the intimidation of someone using a mobile phone, such as the sending of abusive calls and text messages

Irish mobile phone firms are offering tips on how to handle telephone bullies who terrorise children. And they are asking parents to discuss the issue of mobile bullying and the sending of offensive material by text or picture messaging (*The Sun*)

mobile wallet *n.* a mobile phone that can be used in making purchases in the same way as a debit or credit card

This adds significance to an announcement, earlier this year, by Vodafone and T-Mobile, who between them control 80% of the Europe's largest mobile market in Germany, and half of the British market. They are working together on an interoperable mobile payments platform and are hoping that other operators will join them. Under this system, a Vodafone subscriber could spend money from their mobile wallet with a T-Mobile merchant (*The Guardian*)

mobisode *n.* a short episode of a television show, intended for viewing on a mobile phone [a blend of MOBILE PHONE and EPISODE]

If you thought the adrenalin-packed adventures of Jack Bauer were draining in a one-hour sitting of 24, wait until a 60-second 'mobisode' is streamed down a mobile phone near you. Illicit sex, murder and identity theft are dispatched at lightning speed in the first bite-size episode of the thriller ... The first of 24 monthly mobisodes does not so much leave you wanting more as needing to view it again, preferably at half-speed. Studying the grainy images, for which subscribers [are expected] to pay £40 a month, on a 2in (5cm) screen is a reminder of why wide-screen home entertainment systems will be flying out of Dixons this Christmas (*The Times*)

mom test *n.* US, *informal* a test of the user-friendliness of a computer device or software based on the extent to which a user's mother is able to use it

Using the 'mom test', I've had my mom add memory and swap cards/drives in her computer, and she's recently even done it without my direction or assistance. Non-technical people can do this stuff, it's just that they don't want to (*SlashDot.com*)

moobs *pl n.* *informal* twin areas of flabby flesh, resembling female breasts, on a man's chest [a contraction of MAN BOOBS]

Hey, I looked everywhere but I really couldn't find it on this website about what exercise or weightlifting helps get rid of chest fat or moobs. If any one could lend any support it would be greatly appreciated. Thank you (*MensHealth.co.uk forums*)

Mother of Satan *n.* a name for triacentone triperoxide (TATP), a highly unstable explosive substance often used by suicide bombers, notably in the 7/7 London attacks

> But as the Palestinian bomb-makers will attest – 40 Palestinians are thought to have been killed making or handling the explosive – it is highly unstable and sensitive to heat and friction. Not for nothing is it known as 'Mother of Satan' (*The Times*)

muffin top *n. informal* a roll of flesh spilling over the top of a tight skirt or trousers, esp when the midriff is exposed [from the similarity of this to a muffin expanding over its case]

> But another part of me is horrified. Dimply, heat-rashed tummies with bottomless belly buttons are not for sharing with the world, I want to yell. ... It's just as well the so-called muffin-top look is going out of style, because in some places like the most conservative of the US, flaunting flesh is likely to be made illegal. In Louisiana, a Bill was lodged under which individuals dressed in pants that expose skin or undies would face a fine of up to $500 and possible jail time (*The Courier-Mail*)

murk *vb. slang* **1** to murder **2** to defeat convincingly

> I got a neighbor who always wants to work on the Sabbath. Exodus 35:2 clearly says he should be murked. Does that mean I gotta murk him myself? (*babyz.sulekha.com*)

> The 1st one when we went to Cleveland it was Me, Hostyle, Killa Khaun, Finale, Moe Dirdee, Nina Da

> Pimp and we went down to Cleveland and ripped some heads open. It got ruled as bein a draw but you know how shit is. They came to Detroit and we murked them, we knocked them out (*detroithiphop.com*)

Murrayfield *n. British, informal* an alternative term for 'Henman Hill', the grassy area in the All England Tennis club in which spectators without tickets for the main courts during the Wimbledon championships congregate to watch matches on a large screen. *Also called* **Murray's Mount** [from Andy Murray (born 1987), a Scottish tennis player seen as a potential British Wimbledon champion; playing on MURRAYFIELD the Scottish national rugby stadium in Edinburgh]

> By yesterday afternoon, when Murray's match against the Argentinian David Nalbandian began, the erstwhile Henman Hill – upon which the more fervent Henmaniacs were once wont to gather – had been rechristened either Murray's Mount or Murrayfield. The crowds were there to roar their support for this twitchy teenage repository of their fresh dreams (*The Telegraph*)

naked street *n.* a traffic-management strategy pioneered in the Netherlands in which all distinctions between pavements and roads are removed. Each road

user is given equal priority, thereby ensuring that
motorists have to slow down and drive more carefully

> Sir, Your report (January 6) on London's first 'naked
> street', stripped of road signs, markings and traffic
> lights, omits one important piece of advice: how to fill
> in the form in the event of having to submit a claim to
> one's motor insurers following an accident. Who had
> the right of way? (*Letter to The Times*)

nang *or* **nanging** *adj. London slang* excellent; cool
[the etymology of *nang* is much disputed: some have
suggested Bengali *nengta* or Hindi *nanga*, 'naked',
while other theories include the Vietnamese *nặng,*
'heavy' and the West African language Mende, via
Jamaican Creole. In its current form, the term seems
to have emerged from UK rap music; one possibility is
that it is simply a corruption of (HAPPE)NING.]

> Me? I'm just jammin wid me bruds. Dis my yard,
> innit? Is nang, you get me? (*The Guardian*)

nanograss *n.* a synthetic surface consisting of minute
upright blades of silicon that allow control of the way it
interacts with liquids

> Bell Labs is betting that nanograss will find its way
> into commercial products ranging from low-friction
> boat hulls to heat sinks for computer processors and

batteries with a shelf life of 25 years (*Computer World*)

nanomedicine *n.* the application of nanotechnology to medicine

> What if doctors could search out and destroy the very first cancer cells that would otherwise have caused a tumor to develop in the body? What if a broken part of a cell could be removed and replaced with a miniature biological machine? What if pumps the size of molecules could be implanted to deliver life-saving medicines precisely when and where they are needed? These scenarios may sound unbelievable, but they are the long-term goals of the NIH Roadmap's Nanomedicine initiative that we anticipate will yield medical benefits as early as 10 years from now. (*National Institutes of Health (US)*)

NASCAR dad *n.* *US* a stereotypical representation of a white working-class American male with a family [from NASCAR a trademark (National Association for Stock Car Racing), a form of motor racing supposedly popular with this type of man]

> Although NASCAR says its audience covers a broad spectrum of America, a stereotype fan has emerged. He is called the NASCAR Dad – white, male, conservative, and southern. The NASCAR dads are said to be a solidly Republican group (*Voice of America (scripted radio news)*)

Who are you?

With marketing people, journalists, and psephologists making their livings from generalizing about our tastes and traits, there's a steady flow of new demographic labels into English. The phenomenon really caught the popular imagination in the 1980s, with the *yuppies* – young upwardly mobile professionals – who set the standard for this kind of word. Thus, in the latest crop, we have **yeppies, yindies,** and **yupsters,** all modelled on *yuppie.*

Not all such terms have the staying power of *yuppie,* of course. *Yindie* and *yupster* are competing for the same territory, and there are other equivalents such as **grup,** *dadster,* and *scenior.* Only one of these is likely to survive to be eclipsed by the next set of labels.

Pinning labels on vast swathes of the population is an inexact science. When David Davis set out his plans to appeal to the **wristband generation** in late 2005, during his bid for the Conservative Party leadership, the fashion for charity bracelets was already waning. Other 'key demographics' beloved of politicians and pollsters, such as **Nascar dads** and **schoolgate mums,** come and go with each election.

Perhaps the demographic labels that we like most are those that don't apply to 'us' – or so we like to think. The ubiquitous *chav* (see **Chavian flu,** p 32) is the best example. As *chav* is an informal word with blatant overtones of snobbery, it's unsurprising that a formal equivalent has sprung into being: the acronym **Neet.** This carries the same pejorative load as *chav,* but sounds matter-of-fact enough to be used more freely.

Neet *n acronym for British, informal* not in education, employment, or training

> A class of uber-chavs, they encompass a wide range of people, from the law abiding who have fallen on hard times, to the truly antisocial neighbours from hell... Aged between 16 and 24, they number 1.1 m and are responsible for a social and economic drag on society that is vastly disproportionate to their numbers. A study by the Department for Education and Skills conservatively estimates that each new Neet dropping out of education at 16 will cost taxpayers an average of £97,000 during their lifetime, with the worst costing more than £300,000 apiece *(The Times)*

negging *n.* the practice of making unflattering comments to a person one is trying to seduce, in the hope that he or she will react by attempting to win one's approval [from NEGATIVE]

> Take the key PUA [pick-up artist] tactic of 'negging', in which, tapping into female insecurity, you offer a woman a line that is both compliment and insult: 'I like your skirt. I just saw another girl wearing the same one a moment ago' *(The Guardian)*

nerdcore *n. music, US, informal* a style of rap music, characterized by lyrics about computer programming and academic study [from NERD + (HARD)CORE]. *See also* **geeksta**

Also dubbed 'nerdcore,' this branch of hip-hop is for geeks, by geeks *(Wired)*

nerdvana *n. informal* a state of great satisfaction or pleasure attained by a nerd when pursuing his or her hobby or interest [a blend of NERD and NIRVANA]

> Danny lifted the receiver and dictated a passphrase of some sort. Presto – the rear wall of the booth opened, and we stepped into – nerdvana. From a cramped phone booth into massive pure-white-lit space two-stories high, adorned with all manner of things strange and beautiful. Over to one side stood the Terminator-like skeleton of a forty-foot dinosaur, its 15-foot pneumatic legs gleaming and exposed … The space was a great big project lab, with happy geeks combing over various assemblages of wiring, motors, processors and plans like ants on a summer picnic. It's Willy Wonka's chocolate factory for geeks *(boingboing.net)*

neuroeconomics *n.* a discipline combining economics, psychology, and neuroscience, that examines how people evaluate decisions, risks, and rewards > **neuroeconomist** *n.*

> The researchers are also finding that money makes us nutty. We should treat money as a mere exchange mechanism that allows us to get stuff. That distinction is lost on our brains. The dopamine release that makes a juicy hamburger so satisfying works the same

magic even if we simply find the money to buy the
burger. There's not much profit yet in
neuroeconomics' eyebrow-raising sidekick
neuromarketing but that might not be far behind
(*The Times*)

neuromarketing *n.* the process of researching the
brain patterns of consumers to reveal their responses
to particular advertisements and products before
developing new advertising campaigns and branding
techniques

Pepsi™ or Coke™? You probably think that your
response to the taste challenge is just that, based on
taste. Neuroscientists, though, are messing with our
heads and shattering these preconceptions. Last year
a US scientist used brain scans to show that both
brands activate the pleasure centres of the brain. This
proves, he claims, that people's cola preferences are
based on factors other than taste – factors such as
brand image and lifestyle associations. The research
has created quite a stir in the business press;
neuromarketing is being touted as the next big thing.
If big business can use science to locate and push
consumers' 'buy buttons', then it can manipulate our
every thought, and its bottom line (*The Times*)

nom de womb *n. informal* a name used by an
expectant parent to refer to their unborn child [a play
on NOM DE PLUME]

I dreamed our baby was a girl, and when I awoke, I
remembered her name, one I've never even heard:
Deanna Fabrice. So, inevitably, Deanna Fabrice has
become the baby's latest nom de womb, as in 'How's
Deanna Fabrice feeling?' and other such insufferable
stuff that would force any but the most tolerant of
souls to leave the room (*Parenting Magazine*)

nonebrity *n. informal, derogatory* a person with
celebrity status, despite seeming to have done very
little to merit it [a blend of NONENTITY and
CELEBRITY]

Listening to the gooey music the festival organisers
have blaring from loudspeakers has become more of a
trial. The same goes for the spectacle of collagen and
silicone-enhanced Euro 'nonebrities' turning out for
the gala premieres, 8ft tall with mahogany tans,
among whom the sweaty and T-shirted international
press scurry like poor relations (*The Guardian*)

nouse *trademark n.* a device which enables the user of
a computer to direct the cursor around the screen by
means of nose movements [a blend of NOSE and
MOUSE]

Using a computer will soon be a lot easier for disabled
people, thanks to a hands-free device created by
Canadian researchers. The 'Nouse,' short for 'nose as
mouse,' is the brainchild of Dmitry Gorodnichy,
research officer at the National Research Council's

Institute for Information Technology. It uses
movements of the tip of the user's nose to direct the
cursor, which is normally controlled by a conventional
mouse. At the beginning of a computer session, an
ordinary Web cam zooms in on the tip of the nose
and takes a snapshot of about 25 pixels. It then mirrors
the nose's movements on screen to move the cursor,
just as a hand would normally move a mouse
(*CNN.com*)

nutrigenomics *pl n.* the study of how food affects
people according to their genetic make-up

If you're already thinking, like many Australians, what
should I do because I'm half Italian and half Scottish,
or half Greek and half Irish, relax. The wizards behind
nutrigenomics say that about 65 per cent of us should
stick with the fruits, vegetables and proteins that form
the basis of good nutrition. Those with the most to
gain from gene-determined diets are the fortunate
few who will discover they really can eat whatever
they want (*The Courier-Mail*)

obesogenic *adj. medical* causing obesity

The power of the 'obesogenic environment' is
apparently such that it disempowers us from making
choices over what we eat, duping us all the time into
thinking that we are making choices when in fact we
are just riding the junk-food wave (*Spiked*)

onshoring *n.* the practice of locating a business in
one's own country (as opposed to abroad)

Information Week: Are you looking to put a stop to offshoring? White: I never said offshoring is bad. I just feel there's also a place for onshoring at a low cost. I believe in a global economy that includes US workers (*InformationWeek*)

Oprahfication *n.* *informal* the perceived increase in people's desire to discuss their emotions or personal problems, attributed to the influence of confessional television programmes [from OPRAH (WINFREY), US chat-show host and pioneer of this genre]

The [Oprah Winfrey] show's trademark mix of inspirational stories and tales of personal redemption led the Wall Street Journal to coin the word Oprahfication to describe public confession as a form of therapy (*News24.com*)

orthorexia *n.* an abnormal interest in the nutritional content of one's food and an aversion to foods containing preservatives or certain types of fat [a blend of ORTHO-, in the sense meaning 'correct or right' and ANOREXIA] > **orthorexic** *n, adj.*

The self-described 'extreme eater' found himself in a hotbed of new-age food theories. He quickly forged his own diet, eating only vegetables just plucked from the ground and chewing each mouthful 50 times. Like many orthorexics, he became increasingly inflexible about his dietary restrictions, ending up on the road

> to a fully-fledged eating disorder similar to anorexia
> and bulimia. He dubbed it 'orthorexia' (*The Herald*)

overclocking *n. computing, informal* the practice of physically modifying a computer so that its processors can run at speeds much greater than the manufacturer intended [from the so-called 'clock' within a processor that controls the speed at which it runs] > **overclocker** *n.*

> Hardcore computer gamers are taking their passion
> to new levels by using car parts and fish tank pumps
> to give them the edge on the virtual battleground. It's
> all part of an underground craze called 'overclocking'
> which allows game players to run their computers at
> twice the speed they were designed for – despite the
> threat of injury to their computers and themselves
> (*The Sunday Mail*)

Padre Pio *n. Irish, slang* **a** a form of punishment shooting employed by paramilitaries in Northern Ireland in which the victim is shot through the palms of both hands **b** (as modifier) *a Padre Pio shooting* [from PADRE PIO (1887-1968), a Capuchin friar said to have borne stigmata on his hands for more than fifty years]

> The second Padre Pio attack happened in January ... A

> gunman shot a youth through both hands, leaving the
> victim with wounds reminiscent of the Italian priest
> venerated for his stigmata (*The Belfast Telegraph*)

pajamahadeen *n. US, informal* a collective term for politically motivated bloggers [from PAJAMA (implying a lack of professionalism; that they write from home as a hobby) + (MUJA)HADEEN (implying guerrilla tactics). The name was coined in response to a statement from Jonathan Klein, a former *60 Minutes* senior executive, in which he suggested that the typical blogger, in contrast to the professional journalist, is 'a guy sitting in his living room in his pajamas']

> Well, last week, the insurrectionary pajama people –
> dubbed 'pajamahadeen' by some Web nuts –
> successfully scaled one more citadel of the
> mainstream media, CBS News. One of the biggest,
> baddest media stars, Dan Rather, is now clinging,
> white-knuckled, to his job. Not bad for a bunch of
> slackers in their nightclothes (*Time Magazine*)

pastorpreneur *n.* (in the US) a preacher who uses methods traditionally associated with business to expand their congregation and attract funding to his ministry [from PASTOR + (ENTRE)PRENEUR]

> In their pursuit of 'total service excellence' America's

pastorpreneurs do not just preach on Sundays and deal with the traditional 'hatch, match and dispatch' rites of passage. They keep their buildings open seven days a week, from dawn to dusk, and deliver a truly catholic array of services. Some mega-church complexes house banks, pharmacies and schools (*The Economist*)

peacocking *n.* the practice of dressing outlandishly as a seduction strategy

Furthermore, the peacocking of these PUAs [pick-up artists] is decidedly hen-like. They wear platform shoes, wigs, fake piercings, frilly shirts, purple furry vests, and even paint their nails. That the women they target are attracted to such trappings makes one wonder why they bother with men in the first place. It seems to me they could find more alluring specimens of femininity and fashion within their own bathroom stalls (*enterstageright.com*)

pebcak *n acronym for* problem exists between chair and keyboard: a jocular term used, esp by those employed in IT, to attribute blame for a problem to the user of the computer rather than the computer itself

…one of the agents was having a problem with his machine. As I walked by in the hallway, I heard, 'Oh, I'm sure Lynnette can fix it, it's probably that PEBCAK error again. Those happen a lot with this system' (*novell.community.chat*)

Here for a day?

Of the thousands of new words that flood into English every year, some will cement themselves in our everyday vocabulary, while others will become specialist terms that experts in particular fields will continue to use. A great many, however, will vanish.

Of the words in this book, for example, **podcasting** is clearly here to stay (at least until some other technology supersedes it), while the **hyote,** alas, is surely doomed to extinction. These, in their different ways, are extreme cases. *Podcasting* is a neat term for a new phenomenon that has become part of everyday life for millions in the last couple of years; the *hyotes* were removed from the cryptozoologist's casebook with the discovery that they were merely balding foxes. But what about the rest of the words in this book? No one can say for sure, but it's a fair bet that a good few of them will be standard inclusions in the dictionaries of the near future.

So what makes a word stick? The simplest answer is that for a word to last, it usually needs to describe something that hasn't been described before. Technology drives language to a remarkable extent; when something new is created, it needs a name. Of course, slang terms often describe things that already have perfectly good names. The key here is for slang or jargon to transcend the limited group in which it is first used. The mass media can help, especially the internet, which has brought a huge amount of technical terminology and geeky jargon into the mainstream – and into the dictionary.

petrosexual *n.* a pet animal that is groomed, pampered, and indulged to a high degree [a blend of PET and METROSEXUAL]. *See* **Sexual advances, page 141**

> Brittany travels regularly between the East and West coasts, often sporting the latest fashions by Oscar Newman, a 'red carpet' staple. She stays in the best hotels and eats in five star restaurants, with a particular penchant for Vietnamese and Thai food. When she does eat dog food, it is only all natural and holistic. She is groomed regularly, and if she needs medical attention, she is only treated by a homeopathic veterinarian. Brittany is a petrosexual (*Asbury Park Press*)

pharmbot *n.* a computerized mechanical device used to dispense prescription drugs [a blend of PHARMACEUTICAL and ROBOT]

> Two pharmacy robots at Christ and University hospitals can fill in patient prescriptions so quickly and accurately that they will soon dole out medications for all six hospitals in the Health Alliance system. The ability to quickly and correctly supply medication is critical in a national health care market where the 3 billion prescriptions filled each year are expected to increase by as much as 18 percent. At the same time, there is a shortage of pharmacists, as reported in the Courier's Nov. 9 issue. The national vacancy rate is 21 percent. Enter the pharmbot (*Cincinnatti Business Courier*)

phone chicken *n.* any game in which a participant stays in a dangerous situation for as long as possible while an accomplice films the proceedings using a camera phone [from the game CHICKEN, the object of which is to make one's opponent lose his or her nerve, and thus be *chicken,* or cowardly]

> Children are filming themselves dicing with death in front of trains – in a deadly craze called phone chicken. Youngsters wait on tracks and then dive out of the way of fast trains at the very last minute as their friends film it on their mobile phones to brag about their dangerous antics (*Channel Four News*)

phonejacker *n.* *informal* person who robs people of their mobile phones, esp in a public place using violence or the threat of violence

> With more mobile phones than cars being stolen in some European cities, right now you're more likely to be the victim of a 'phonejacker' than a hacker (*Time Magazine*)

phone spamming *n.* the practice of sending automated telephone messages promising prizes or bargains, the claiming of which requires the caller to phone costly premium-rate numbers > **phone spammer** *n.*

More than six million people have tried to protect
their mobile and home telephones from increasing
intrusion by 'phone spammers' who cold-call
customers with often bogus offers of holidays and
cash prizes running to tens of thousands of pounds.
But the evasive manoeuvre is failing to stop the
growing industry which offers the 'prizes' if the
recipient dials a number beginning 090 – at a
premium rate of up to £1.50 a minute (*The Guardian*)

phonetography *n.* the art of taking photographs with
a camera phone [a blend of PHONE and
PHOTOGRAPHY]

THE TIMES PHONETOGRAPHY CHALLENGE.
Camera phones used to take notoriously awful, fuzzy
pictures, but things have moved on. With the latest
mobile handsets, many now with megapixel cameras,
it's possible to take great pictures good enough for
publication in print and online (*The Times*)

piking *n.* *British*, *slang* the practice of deriving sexual
pleasure from watching strangers have sex in parked
cars and other secluded but public places

High wages and a lack of discipline from those in
control of the game have helped create a sordid off-
the-field culture of immorality, decadence and
thuggery, of roasting, dogging and piking (*The Sun*)

pimp up *slang* *vb.* to customize (a vehicle) with

special features and ostentatious decorations
> **pimped-up** *adj.* [from the extravagant customized car typically owned by a PIMP]

> Sean Coombes, P Diddy, Puff Daddy, Duff Paddy, or whatever he's calling himself at the moment, is releasing his own range of 'pimped-up' cars. If you have £100,000 to spare you can bid on eBay for a Sean John Lincoln Navigator with all the bling a badboy rapper wannabe (or Premiership footballer) could need. J-Lo's ex has customized the 4x4 with crazy 'extras' only a bored man could dream up (*The Sun*)

pixiecam *n.* a very small digital camera

> This is the multipurpose PixieCam I always wanted but never got. The battery case cover is flimsy and prone to coming off. The best part is that it uses AAA batteries – no difficulty replacing power when you are far from an outlet (*good-music-guide.com*)

playlist anxiety *n.* worry or apprehension about what other people will think of the music held on one's MP3 player

> With the ease of sharing playlists via iTunes™ or other music software, it appears that some listeners freak out over what others might think of their music-listening tastes, and some even change what they listen to in such environments to protect how others might view them. Apparently, that concept is interesting enough that some researchers are doing a

study of how playlist anxiety impacts people in an
office environment (*stargeek.com*)

podfading *or* **podfade** *n.* **1** the tendency of new
podcasters to stop producing podcasts after an initial
period of enthusiasm **2** an instance of this
> **podfader** *n.* [a blend of (I)POD a trademark and
FADING coined by US podcaster Scott Fletcher]

> Frank McMahon, who produces or hosts five podcasts,
> worries that podfading will kill off some of the
> medium's freshest, most unusual voices. After
> watching a recent episode of *Four-Eyed Monsters,* a
> video podcast in which the hosts spotlighted their
> own exhaustion and frustration with the craft,
> McMahon recorded a special audio edition for their
> RSS stream to encourage them to keep going
> (*wired.com*)

podnography *n.* pornographic podcasts or vodcasts
[a blend of (I)POD a trademark and PORNOGRAPHY]
> **podnographer** *n. Compare* **sexcast**

> One of the most successful exponents of
> podnography is a London student known as Faceless
> (she of the sexual stamina and melting chocolate).
> Her accounts of her sex life with her boyfriend and
> her bit on the side have made her the most popular
> podcaster on both sides of the Atlantic. Unusually for
> a podnographer, Faceless does not record her
> broadcasts herself. She dictates them and an actress

reads them, for that extra degree of distance from her fans (*The Observer*)

podosphere *n.* *informal* the world's podcasts viewed collectively; the podcasting milieu [from (i)POD a trademark + SPHERE; modelled on BLOGOSPHERE]

> The podosphere may be virgin terrain for the online world, but already the race is on to figure out whether there's any real money to be made through the new medium (*Wired*)

podsafe *adj.* (of music, etc) licensed for use in podcasting irrespective of other licensing restrictions that may apply > **podsafety** *n.*

> Podcatching software such as Apple's iTunes™ allows us to subscribe to shows, which are then automatically downloaded as they appear online so that we can listen at our leisure, dipping in, rewinding and repeating at will. This gives the music industry a headache, because the licences normally granted to broadcasters simply don't cover this new format. As a result, the majority of podcasts are dominated by uncensored, rambling speech – the audio equivalent of the average blog – and any music that is featured must be 'podsafe' – ie doesn't fall under a standard record-label agreement (*The Independent*)

podslurping *n.* the use of portable media devices, such as MP3 players or USB sticks, to steal confidential

business data

> 'Podslurping' is a recently coined term that refers to the ability of iPods™ to steal business information right out of the network. Of course, iPods aren't the only devices that can easily be plugged into USB data and used to download gigabytes of data; there are also USB sticks, MP3 players, digital cameras and assorted CD devices (*Image and Data Manager Magazine*)

poptronica *n.* pop music created using synthesizers, samplers, etc, rather than traditional instruments [a blend of POP and ELECTRONICA]

> From a corner of his bedroom comes the not remotely lo-fi poptronica of Bitmap. A little bit Lemon Jelly, a little bit Zombies, Alpha Beta Gamma is a delight. Basically, it's the album we've all been hoping the Beta Band would make. Smart electronic noodling underpins old-school melodic pop that veers from easy listening to weird psychedelic workouts (*The Times*)

pop-up shop *n.* *Another name for* guerrilla store

> When friends came back from Japan with bags of funky accessories, graphic designer Chloe Quigley knew just how to move some units for them – set up a pop-up shop. The day before the sale, she posted an email notice to the 3000 subscribers [to her website], letting them know about a new store, open for the last three days of July in the empty site of [an] old boutique, which had just moved. Ms Quigley thought

the pop-up shop concept would work: even though it wasn't a clearance store, she was confident the shoppers would run in if they thought they only had one weekend before the whole shop disappeared (*The Age*)

pornaoke *n.* an entertainment in which members of an audience emit lustful utterances in synchronization with a pornographic film shown silently on a large screen [a blend of PORN and KARAOKE]

> The city can now boast not only licensed saunas and sex shops, as well as a well-known high street purveyor of sex toys on Princes Street itself, but a growing number of strip bars and pubs offering lapdancing, plus an erotic cinema and a Festival of Erotica. Now a city nightclub is to host an event called Pornaoke, which encourages members of the public to add their own 'sound effects' to silent clips of sex scenes from pornographic films (*Edinburgh Evening News*)

porno sir *n. informal* a teacher who has been convicted of, or cautioned for, viewing child pornography, esp one who has been permitted to continue teaching by the authorities

> Straight after this interview, Johnson is off to 'doughnut' in the Commons – sit alongside his colleagues for the benefit of the television cameras – as Ruth Kelly, the education secretary, makes her

statement on sex offenders. While he is scathing about the confusion of her performance the week before – 'if she thinks there is a case for allowing repentant sex offenders to be gym teachers, well she should have the guts to say so' – he is also dismissive of the hysteria about 'porno sirs' (*The Guardian*)

pram face *n. British, derogatory, slang* a young woman whose appearance and demeanour supposedly recall those of a young mother wheeling a pram around a deprived area

Imagine the black equivalent of Vicky Pollard, hilarious though she is – we just wouldn't let ourselves laugh. And what would the equivalent of the prole-girl name-calling – 'pram-face', 'chip-shop' – be? Curry-face, corner-shop? You'd feel the long arm of the CRE on your shoulder in no time (*The Times*)

pranking *n. British, informal* the practice of phoning a person and putting the phone down before they answer. This results in the person feeling obliged to return the call, which ensures that the original caller enjoys a conversation without paying for the call

Unlike the Italians who ring once to flirt or convey the message 'I'm thinking about you.' UK Teenagers ring once to save money. In what they call 'pranking', they dial a number and hang up after the first ring, so their number appears on the cell screen of the recipient, who then calls them back at his expense (*textually.org*)

pretox *n.* **1** a method of dealing with expected alcoholic and culinary excesses by eating and drinking healthily in advance | *vb.* **2** to employ such a method [a blend of PRE- and DETOX]

> According to Dr John Briffa, we're never going to go an entire month on wheat grass and whole foods alone. Much better to pretox – balance the bad we do to our bodies with pre-emptive nutrients and compensatory behaviour (*The Observer*)

prison-white *adj.* *British*, *informal* (of training shoes) spotlessly white, as if having been worn only indoors, esp in prison [from the perhaps misguided assumption that it is impossible to soil one's footwear in prison]

> Michael Douglas's missus is usually all Hollywood glitz and glamour. But the screen siren has obviously been influenced by her time with fellow Welsh lass and chav idol Charlotte. Catherine ditched her super-expensive frocks and heels for a puffa jacket and prison-white trainers (*The Sun*)

privocrat *n.* *US* (esp in neo-conservative thought) a person who is not in favour of relinquishing individual freedoms in order to give the state more powers to combat terrorism [a blend of PRIVACY and -CRAT, modelled on TECHNOCRAT, etc]

> The privocrats only grudgingly acknowledge that
> terrorism exists, and they never concede that a gain in
> the public good may justify a concession in 'privacy'
> (*City Journal*)

pro-ana *adj.* **1** of or related to the belief that anorexia nervosa is a valid lifestyle choice rather than an disorder | *n.* **2** an internet-based community that advocates anorexia nervosa as a valid lifestyle choice [a contraction of *pro-anorexia,* with the *ana* element imitating a girl's name]. *Compare* **pro-mia.** *See also* **thinspiration**

> The actress and singer says she used pro-ana sites
> while suffering from anorexia. Her illness got so bad,
> she had to enter rehab and leave the set of *Reba*, the
> TV show she starred in alongside Reba McEntire. She
> is now in recovery and is an ambassador for the
> National Eating Disorders Association (*CNN.com*)

promatorium *n.* a building in which corpses are frozen at extremely low temperatures so that they can be reduced to powder [a blend of PROMESSION (the process of reducing a body to powder) and CREMATORIUM]

A town in Sweden plans to become the first place in the world where corpses will be disposed of by freeze-drying, as an environmentally friendly alternative to cremation or burial. Jonkoping, in southern Sweden, is to turn its crematorium into a so-called promatorium next year. Swedes will then have the chance to bury their dead according to the pioneering method, which involves freezing the body, dipping it in liquid nitrogen and gently vibrating it to shatter it into powder (*The Daily Telegraph*)

pro-mia *adj.* **1** of or relating to the belief that bulimia nervosa is a valid lifestyle choice rather than a disorder | *n.* **2** an internet-based community that advocates bulimia nervosa as a valid lifestyle choice [a contraction of *pro-bulimia,* with the *mia* element imitating a girl's name]. *Compare* **pro-ana.** *See also* **thinspiration**

These insidious sites offer 'support and guidance' to anorexics and bulimics, encouraging them to put their lives at risk. The websites, known as either pro-ana (pro-anorexia) or pro-mia (pro-bulimia), have mushroomed in the past few years with names like I Love You to the Bones, Hungry for Perfection, the Art of Reduction, and Living on Oxygen, and they use encouragement and the fear of disapproval to reinforce their power (*The Mail on Sunday*)

property porn *n. British, informal* a genre of escapist

TV programmes, magazine features, etc, showing desirable properties for sale, esp those in idyllic rural locations, aimed at providing vicarious pleasure rather than attracting buyers

> Thus those of us flat out on the sofa after a week's honest toil face a bleak choice: slow death by David Jason on ITV, property porn on Five, or a lame mixture of sitcom and gardening from the Beeb (*The Sun*)

puddle phishing *n.* a form of phishing that is targeted at customers of small financial institutions [from PHISHING: the practice of using fraudulent e-mails and copies of legitimate websites to extract financial data from computer users for purposes of identity theft; itself playing on FISHING, hence the idea of fishing in a small pool, or PUDDLE]

> Phishers are baiting users of smaller banks, a security firm says, calling the practice 'puddle phishing' (*informationweek.com*)

pyromarketing *n.* a marketing technique that relies on product recommendations by trusted or authoritative figures [from PYRO-, denoting fire, because this marketing approach is supposed to 'ignite' sales]

Mr Gibson promoted 'The Passion' by talking to prominent religious figures, who then encouraged their flocks to purchase large blocks of tickets. 'The Purpose Driven Life' became a best-seller because it became a staple of church sermons and church study-groups. Greg Stielstra, formerly Zondervan's chief marketing man (who has to his name 88 best-sellers, 20 number-one best-sellers and eight books that have sold more than 1m copies), calls this 'pyromarketing'. Rather than promoting people and goods through mass-market media such as television, pyromarketing relies on 'consumer evangelists' who spread the word among like-minded people (*The Economist*)

rainbow party *n. chiefly US and Canadian* a possibly mythical group-sex act, allegedly popular amongst teenagers, in which female participants wear different-coloured lipsticks and fellate male participants in sequence, to different depths [from the supposed bands of colour left on the penises of male participants]

Ms Penny said she talks both to parents who assume that since oral sex wasn't on the radar when they were teens, their kids aren't considering it either, and to young girls who are taking part in 'rainbow parties' in which a series of girls each perform oral sex on several boys (*Chronicle-Herald*)

raunch culture *n.* the practices and attitudes that

promote overtly sexual representations of women, as through the acceptance of pornography, stripping, breast implants, and skimpy clothing, esp as advanced and accepted by women

> Take Jenna Jameson. The world's most popular adult film performer, she has proved to be one of raunch culture's most effective proselytisers. Her memoir, *How to Make Love Like a Porn Star,* spent six weeks on *The New York Times* bestseller list last year. In it, Jameson writes that 'being in the industry can be a great experience' because 'you can actually become a role model for women' (*The Sydney Morning Herald*)

read dating *n.* an activity similar to speed dating in which participants wear a name tag that also displays their favourite book title as an indication of their suitability as potential romantic partners [a play on SPEED DATING]

> The only thing preventing me is that this event is not an ordinary speed dating occasion, all beer and bells and braying chat-up lines. This is 'read dating' and after half a glass of wine my companions start to look less like terrifying predators and more like the sort of pleasant, slightly shy types that, well, you'd expect to meet in a library on a quiet Thursday night (*The Guardian*)

reality mining *or* **reality browsing** *n.* the creation and exploitation of a vast dataset of human behaviour to provide quickly accessible information on social systems and interaction

> Think of 'reality mining' as a supercharged version of the presence-management abilities of the AOL Buddy List. The Buddy List gives you one or two simple bits of information about your posse: Who's online? And if they've been dormant, how long? This lets you get a nigh-tactile sense of the current status of your friends, almost as if you were able to glance around the room and look at everyone. Now imagine your buddy list were able to track all sorts of other things: where your spouse's car currently is (and how fast it's travelling), where your kids are (and who they're with), how busy each of the local restaurants are, and which bank machine near you has the biggest lineup. It's sort of like having ESP (*collisiondetection.net*)

reBay *vb.* to resell something previously bought on the eBay website [a play on EBAY a trademark]

> Let's see, I could spend hours on the phone failing to find a replacement rear triangle for my Schwinn Rocket 88, eventually paying way too much for one, or I can go to ebay and buy a used Schwinn for the parts, reBaying the parts I don't need (*dirtragmag.com*)

reboot *informal vb.* **1** to abandon continuity in a fictional story line such as a comic-book or TV series | *n.* **2** a new version of an existing comic-book, TV series, etc, which makes no reference to the earlier version

> ... any creator who is not working on a reboot is not worth his weight in spice. Why work on some tired old continuity, striving in vain to make it interesting when it is so much easier to throw all the rules out the window and make the character distinctly your own? (*Hal Roth in SilverBulletComics.com*)

> Well, after reading Hal Roth's column, all I can say is what utter rubbish. The reboot is the last resort of the desperate. Rarely is it needed, and mostly it can and should be easily avoided (*SilverBulletComics.com*)

retail politics *n.* *informal* the soliciting of members of the public for votes by a politician in person

> Ahmadinejad's ardent professions of solidarity with workaday Iranians defined his dark-horse campaign a year ago. But once in office, he took retail politics to a whole new level. The visit to Arak in mid-May was his 13th trip to the provinces, each time dragging along his cabinet in the name of bringing the government to the people (*The Washington Post*)

retcon *n.* **1** the process by which a comic, book, TV series, film, etc, reveals information about previously established characters or situations which radically changes the interpretation of the earlier stories | *vb.* **2** to effect this process [from RET(ROACTIVE) +

136

> I don't have a problem with the retcon of Superboy. With Luthor's abilities and resources, putting false information in the Cadmus Project would be easy. If Oracle could do it, so could Luthor (*DC Comics message board*)

reveal party *n. chiefly US* a party held to celebrate successful cosmetic treatment, esp cosmetic surgery or dentistry

> Now the ABC reality show *Extreme Makeover* plans to transform the since-exonerated Krone, once dubbed the "snaggletooth killer," into a man with a winning smile … He's allowed to talk to his family during the procedure … A 'reveal party' is being planned for Krone near his hometown (*The Arizona Republic*)

revirgination *n.* the surgical procedure in which a woman's hymen is artificially restored, usually for cultural reasons

> 'Revirgination' costs as little as $1,800 at Ridgewood Health and Beauty Center, a spa and cosmetic-surgery center in the New York City borough of Queens. To promote the procedure, the center's owner, Cuban-born Esmeralda Vanegas, has given away hymenoplasties on a Spanish-language radio station. She also promotes them in her eponymous magazine, *Esmeralda* (*post-gazette.com*)

ringxiety *n. informal* the anxiety felt by people who hear a mobile phone ringing with a similar ringtone to their own [a blend of RING and ANXIETY]

> Many of us will be familiar with the basest form of ringxiety – when one phone rings and everyone in the vicinity suddenly starts checking their pockets or handbags with frantic abandon. But some cases become far more complex: individuals have reported hearing their phone ring at concerts, or while driving (*The Guardian*)

robotiquette *n.* the rules programmed into or assimilated by a robot that enable it to interact more easily with humans [a blend of ROBOT and ETIQUETTE]

> Robots are learning lessons on 'robotiquette' – how to behave socially – so they can mix better with humans. By playing games, like pass-the-parcel, a University of Hertfordshire team is finding out how future robot companions should react in social situations. The study's findings will eventually help humans develop a code of social behaviour in human-robot interaction (*BBC Online*)

rockonomics *n.* the economics of the music industry, especially with regard to the relationship between music sales and concert ticket prices [from ROCK + (EC)ONOMICS]

> Celine Dion, for example, outearned Rod Stewart in

the rockonomics survey. Krueger and Connolly [the authors of the report] asked, 'On what objective, cardinal metric is Celine Dion only slightly more talented than Rod Stewart?' Hey, the economist who can find some 'objective, cardinal metric' that proves Celine Dion possesses any talent at all should be nominated for a Nobel Prize (*Slate*)

rod from God *n. informal* a weapon, currently in the development stage, that consists of a metal cylinder that is fired from an orbiting spacecraft at a target on earth. The cylinder is calculated to reach speeds in excess of 7000 mph, hitting its target with the power of a small atomic weapon

As now imagined in the Pentagon, 22nd-century 'gunboat diplomacy' will be conducted by what the Air Force's Space Command refers to as 'space-based platforms,' and the cannons of the future will be a range of exotic space weapons and delivery systems, including the so-called Rods from God – tungsten rods launched from orbiting platforms and guided by satellites to pierce hardened bunkers anywhere on Earth … Far from being aimed solely at the protection of US space capabilities, experts believe such weapons are instead intended for offensive, first-strike missions (*The San Francisco Chronicle*)

root causer *n.* (in US neo-conservative thought) a person who believes that Islamic terrorism is a direct result of the foreign policies, particularly those on Israel, Iraq, and Afghanistan, of the US and its closest allies

> It was by no means inevitable that Blair would find himself as the leader of an isolated minority insisting that nothing must change. His initial response after 9/11 was a model of the sort of approach many of his critics are now demanding, including, as he put it to the Labour conference in Brighton two weeks after, 'justice and prosperity for the poor and dispossessed'. If he were to deliver that speech today, he would be denounced as a 'root causer' and an apologist for terrorism (*The Guardian*)

ruralsexual *n. jocular* a type of man, posited to exist in rural areas, with little or no interest in his appearance, in stark contrast to the METROSEXUAL

> As far as Saddam is concerned, some will say he was dirty and disheveled, so how could he be a metrosexual? But that's the modern look. A great deal of grooming is required to look like a complete derelict. In the old days, a person like myself could look like a slob for nothing, but today jeans must be pre-ripped by experts and hair needs a $100 session at the salon to be made to look like a bird-nesting area. Of course, it is true Saddam was living on a farm outside a metro area, and ruralsexual hasn't entered the language until this moment. But Saddam thought he was on vacation, albeit a cut-rate one short on amenities (*post-gazette.com*)

Sexual advances

One persistent linguistic trend over the last decade or so has been the coining of new words to describe various classifications of men. Changing notions of masculinity resulted in the term 'New Man' in the 1980s, but the phenomenon gained momentum with British journalist Mark Simpson and his identification of the *metrosexual* in *The Independent* in 1994. The term remained fairly obscure until Simpson wrote a second article, this time for US web magazine Salon.com in 2002, after which a stream of copycat terms began to spring up on websites and newspapers. Thus we have had *retrosexuals* (also coined by Simpson), **ruralsexuals, technosexuals, petrosexuals, ubersexuals,** and now **heteropolitans.**

Simpson described the meterosexual as a man who has 'taken himself as his own love object and pleasure as his sexual preference'. The term has often been roughly designated as describing a straight man who has adopted the grooming habits more commonly associated with gay men. But what's interesting about *meterosexual* and its derivatives is the way the words are formed. *Metrosexual* appears to be a blend of *metropolitan* and *heterosexual.* But the words derived from *metrosexual* can only be properly understood in reference to it. In these words, the *-sexual* element really means just 'man' – a good example of the shifting, allusive, and inventive nature of contemporary English.

sadfab *n. informal* a single woman, esp one approaching middle age, who is extremely eager to have a baby before she is too old [acronym for 'single and desperate for a baby']

> The one thing that unites all of us reluctant sadfabs is that we've forced ourselves to face the gritty possibility of a life without children – and rejected it out of hand. Rejected it after years of worry, of monitoring our menstrual cycles, of anguished debate with family and friends, of reading every IVF triumph and tragedy in the media, of fearful financial calculation (*The Times*)

scambaiting *n. computing, slang* the practice of pretending to fall for fraudulent online schemes in order to waste the time of the perpetrators

> scambaiter

> The Nigerian scammer Prince Joe Eboh must rue the day that he sent an e-mail to Mike, a PC engineer from Manchester, offering him a cut of $25 million blocked in a Lagos bank account. For Mike is no ordinary PC engineer: he is probably the world's most successful 'scambaiter'. Joe (almost certainly not his real name) and Mike (who never gives his last name) started to correspond, with Mike posing as Father Hector Barnett, the gullible bursar of the fictitious Holy Church of the Order of the Red Breast. Five months later, when the e-mails dried up, Joe was a fully-fledged church member, his breast painted red

to prove his adherence, and $129 poorer (*The Times*)

scanlation *n.* the process of electronically scanning Japanese or Korean manga comics and then translating them into English [a blend of SCAN and TRANSLATION]

> But if the internet has taught us anything, it's that there is no obstacle too difficult for determined hackers to overcome. Welcome to the world of open-source manga – otherwise known as scanlation. The term is a Web-based neologism; a portmanteau word that fuses scan and translation. It's a buzzword you have to be in the know to know, but plugging it into Google produces nearly 11,000 hits. That fact alone is an indication of the breadth of this phenomenon, which is to commercially translated manga what Linux™ is to Windows™ – a collectively generated alternative supported by a thriving and passionate community, produced as a labor of love and distributed for free download via the internet (*sfgate.com*)

school-gate mum *n.* *British* a young family-oriented working mother, considered by political parties as forming a significant part of the electorate [from the fact that such women are to be seen congregating at school gates every afternoon, waiting to take their children home]

The boy started crying when Mr Brown picked him up outside a school in Peckham, South London. He had to hand the one-year-old to fellow minister Harriet Harman. The Chancellor was campaigning to win over 'school-gate mums' – working women voters with kids (*The Sun*)

season creep *n.* the gradual changes in the length of seasons (as demonstrated, for example, by earlier spring weather, flowering of plants, etc), thought to be caused by climate change

The sound of a robin's first song and the sight of young buds on a lilac bush may excite Canadians. But, each year these signs of spring come earlier... It turns out that over the last few years those few extra degrees we've been getting sooner than ever after winter are part of an overall 'season creep' that's bringing home the robin and helping the buds bloom sooner than normal (*Discovery Channel (Canada)*)

set-jetting *n.* the practice of visiting places used as locations in feature films > **set-jetter** *n.* [a spoonerizing play on JET-SETTING]

More than a quarter of Britons say they have chosen a holiday destination after seeing it in a movie or a TV show, or having read about in a book. The biggest beneficiary of set-jetting had been New Zealand after the success of the *Lord Of The Rings films*, research from Halifax Travel Insurance found (*The Scotsman*)

144

sexcast *n.* a sexually explicit podcast or vodcast. *See also* **podnography** [a blend of SEX and (POD)CAST]

> In June, you filthy iTunes™-loving animals made Violet Blue's sexcast – a program that aims 'to be as indecent as possible' – vastly more popular than podcasts from ESPN, the New York Times or MTV's Adam Curry. Congratulations, perverts (*weeklydig.com*)

sheeple *n. informal* people who tend to follow the majority in matters of opinion, taste, etc [a blend of SHEEP and PEOPLE]

> Hollywood has pretty much set themselves up for this, with all the crappy movies they let out the door yearly. I'll wait for the DVD and rent. They get minimum $$ out of my pocket, which is my goal. Most of the sheeple don't have the willpower to do so, sadly. (*slashdot.org*)

shiterature *n.* books, magazines, or newspapers kept in the lavatory to be read while defecating [a blend of SHIT and LITERATURE]

> What made me think that I would read a golfing textbook called 'Following Through'? Actually, that was a bright idea to have a bookcase in the toilet with various punning scatological titles. Fortunately, the joke ended there because I was buggered if I was going to spend time and money finding books with titles like 'Touching Cloth', which if it exists is surely some manner of fashion and fabrics manual. Besides,

I'm not one of life's ruminative pooers, which negates the need for shiterature, unlike most of the Shanahans who spend three-fifths of their lives dumping. Honestly, you'd think we ate nothing but cement for the sheer length of time it takes (*Student Direct*)

shizzle *adj.* **1** a slang word for *sure* used esp by US rappers and their imitators | *n.* **2** a slang word for *shit* used esp by US rappers and their imitators [by using the all-purpose suffix -IZZLE to replace the last element in the original word; this form of slang was popularized by the rappers Snoop Dogg and E-40]

The last time Snoop Dogg came to England, he was met by a newspaper headline saying 'Kick This Evil Bastard Out'. Twelve years on, his situation has changed enormously, Snoop has almost become the gangsta rapper you could take to meet your mother. Fo shizzle, as the man himself might inscrutably say, it's been a long strange trip (*The Guardian*)

shocklog *n.* a deliberately provocative or outrageous blog [a blend of SHOCK and WEBLOG]

Don't get me wrong: it's not a bad thing to be interested in porn, celebrities, funny videos, shocklogs or other time killers. After all, that's what the internet in 2006 is about. But don't get carried away, and spend one hour on trying to download the latest Colin Farrell video. If you really need it in your life, it will come to you. Believe me *(blog.thesedays.com)*

shoulder surfing *n. informal* the practice of looking over the shoulders of someone standing at a cash machine in order to obtain their PIN number

> As revealed in Friday's *Herald Sun,* at least one man has been involved in several Melbourne thefts using the card-trapping devices, which sit in the card slot of an ATM and trap the victim's card. In a method known as 'shoulder surfing', the thief or thieves then trick the victim into trying to retrieve the card by punching in their PIN. The card is not ejected and when the victim leaves the thief removes the device and card in it. The thief then usually goes to another ATM and uses the card and PIN *(Melbourne Herald Sun)*

silent disco *n.* a form of music event at which the music is broadcast to wireless headphones worn by the attendees, thereby ensuring that those in the vicinity of the event are not troubled by noise pollution

> The idea for the silent disco was thought up by [Glastonbury organiser] Eavis' daughter Emily, and the festival will use technology developed by a Dutch company who pioneered headphones for illegal parties that allows clubbers to set their own volume individually. 'Now Emily has finally got something together so the party can go on later into the evening without infringing the noise curfew' explained Eavis

of the new measures. 'It's a first for us, and I will be interested to see how it works' (*New Musical Express*)

Simlish *n.* an invented language used in *The Sims trademark* series of computer games, and in song lyrics by various popular bands [on the model of other blends of ENGLISH, such as CHINGLISH, JAPLISH, and HINGLISH]

> Deh dah do. Misbalah. Que-moh-nuzhnee? Esta booka-dee schvallow en dough cheeky-a-vunch. Don't quite recognise it? It's Simlish, allegedly a combination of fractured Ukrainian and Tagalog, the language of the Philippines, and it could help 80s icons Depeche Mode appeal to a new audience. The Mode, as they are known to fans, have re-recorded one of their singles in the so-called language used by characters in the hugely popular computer game series *The Sims™*, which allows people to build their own cities and worlds (*The Guardian*)

sket *n. British, derogatory, youth slang* a promiscuous girl or woman [of uncertain origin]

> The problem isn't just that Dizzee's East London accent is thick, though it is. It's that Dizzee (ne Dylan Mills), 19, speaks in a tangled local idiom in which choppah means knife, chaps are chains and sket means slut (*Time Magazine*)

skinvertising *n.* a form of advertising in which people are paid to have a company logo or slogan tattooed onto their skin > **skinvertiser** *n.*

> It turns out that if I wanted to be as successful as Fischer, I'd need to think about getting my fringe cut, maybe do something about that ugly scar over my left eyebrow. Such is the price of 'skinvertising', the online fad that last year allowed Fischer to charge $37,375 (£21,200) just for getting a tattoo of a pharmaceutical company's slogan. On his forehead (*The Times*)

slacktivism *n.* the public proclaiming of one's political beliefs through activities that require little effort or commitment, such as attending charity concerts, wearing awareness wristbands, and taking part in short-term boycotts > **slacktivist** *n.* [a blend of SLACKER and ACTIVISM]

> January of this year, the day of President Bush's inauguration, was also the occasion for a novel form of protest against the President and the war in Iraq. 'Not One Damn Dime Day' was, according to its sponsors, an opportunity to speak out against the war by boycotting all forms of consumer spending for 24 hours. 'Open your mouth', their electronic missives implored, 'by keeping your wallet closed'. In its injunction to sit at home and be a tightwad for the day, the Not One Damn Dime Day campaign was an exercise in militant slacktivism. Slacktivism, the phrase itself a rather lazy haemorrhaging of the two words slacker and activism, is the counter-intuitive

idea that you can somehow change the world and
topple its complacent political classes without even
rising from your chair *(The Times)*

slummy mummy *n.* a mother, esp of young children,
who does not live up to media-propagated standards
of attractiveness, healthy living, or good behaviour
[from SLUM and MUMMY; modelled on YUMMY MUMMY:
an attractive woman who has had children]

We drink. We smoke. We're not perfect. We're …
slummy mummies. A generation of women has
decided that just because you've got children doesn't
mean having to live up to an ideal *(The Independent)*

smartmob *n.* a large group of people that is able to
exhibit surprising cohesion and organization through
the use of mobile telephony and the internet [SMART +
MOB influenced by MOB- for *mobile phone*]

The religious smartmob has apparently come of age.
Associate editor Najla Al Rostamani of gulfnews.com
opines: I had first come to realise that the Danish
cartoons debacle would snowball into a controversy
when my mobile phone beeped with the first SMS
message on the issue. This was followed by a second
and a third and a fourth beep. Almost all of them
carried the same message which read as follows:
'Voice your protest to the blasphemous attack on the
prophet (PBUH) and respond by sending a letter of

complaint to Jyllands-Posten.' (*synthesist.blogspot.com*)

smirting *n. informal* flirting between people who are smoking cigarettes outside a no-smoking office, pub, etc > **smirt** *vb.* [a blend of SMOKING and FLIRTING]

> But the smirting scene presents the perils of any dating forum – unwanted attention. Dragging on a Marlboro outside a bar in the West Village, a forty-two-year-old man recalled when he was approached outside another bar by a man wearing a white cowboy hat, western boots, and a huge handlebar moustache (*Columbia News Service*)

sniffing *n. computing, informal* another word for keylogging, a covert practice in which a computer user's keystrokes are monitored by a remote computer

> Keylogging involves using a piece of software – or a piece of hardware – to monitor and record every keystroke entered at a computer terminal, including its time and date. That includes passwords, credit card details and, in one celebrated case, the entire source code for a high-profile computer game. It's also sometimes known as 'sniffing' (*The Times*)

snowclone *n.* a verbal formula that is adapted for reuse by changing only a few words so that the allusion to the original phrase remains clear [coined by Glen Whitman on 15 January 2004; from SNOW, in reference to the common formula 'If the Eskimos have *N* words for snow, then surely *X* have *Y* words for *Z*'; and CLONE, alluding to the replication of the original phrase]. *See also* **Attack of the snowclones, page 155**

> I saw a variant on mrflip's post title recently. It was in a discussion pointing out the massive proliferation of phrases such as 'I, for one, welcome our new *X* overlords' on the internet. (For those who don't recognize, it is a *Simpsons*™ quote). There are lots of phrases like this that people have tweaked and put on their weblogs or in the entertainment section of the newspaper. Examples include '*X* is the new black' and 'Dammit, Jim, I'm a doctor not a *X*.' Well, some language nerds decided to give the phenomenon a name: *snowclone.* Should make it easier to look up discussion about it in the future (*alkalineearth.com*)

snowflake baby *n.* a baby born as a result of the 'adoption' of a frozen embryo for in vitro fertilization [a term coined by the Nightlight Christian Adoptions agency, alluding to the frozen embryos]

> They were the first couple to adopt frozen embryos, and in 1998, their daughter was the first snowflake baby born. In testimony before a subcommittee of the House Committee on Government Reform in July 2001, [Mrs X] spoke out against the use of embryos in stem cell research, and said, 'Any woman can carry an

embryo; tissue or blood matching is not necessary. As embryo adoption proliferates in the wake of this controversy, the 'excess supply' of embryos will evaporate' (*CBS News*)

snubfin, snubfin dolphin *or* **Australian snubfin dolphin** *n.* a species of dolphin, *Orcaella heinsohni,* with a small stubby dorsal fin, a dark dorsal area, lighter brown body and white underbelly, found mainly in Australian waters; identified in 2005

A team of scientists has identified a new dolphin species – the first for at least 30 years – off north Australia. The mammals – named snubfin dolphins – were initially thought to be members of the Irrawaddy species, also found in Australian waters. But one researcher found the snubfins were coloured differently and had different skull, fin and flipper measurements to the Irrawaddys (*BBC*)

sockpuppet *n.* an pseudonymous extra online identity created by a member of an internet discussion forum, etc, to agree with his or her posts, etc, thus giving the impression of support for his or her opinions [by analogy with a puppeteer holding a conversation with the sock puppet on his hand] > **sockpuppeteer** *n.* > **sockpuppetry** *n. See also* **meatpuppet**

> A fifteen year-old boy takes a contract out on his own life and uses sockpuppets to convince another online chat member to murder him (*macminute.com*)

sofa surfing *n.* *informal* the practice of homeless people staying temporarily with various friends and family members while attempting to find more permanent accommodation of their own

> Homelessness charity Crisis warned the phenomenon of 'sofa-surfing', where homeless people move from one friend's house to another, meant many local authorities were unaware how many vulnerable people needed help. Research by the Countryside Agency and Crisis in Craven, North Yorkshire, found only half the homeless people staying with friends and family had applied for local authority help (*BBC Online*)

songlifting *n.* *chiefly US* the practice of downloading music illegally [modelled on SHOPLIFTING]
> **songlifter** *n.*

> 'The theft of music continues to hurt our industry as a whole – from songwriters losing their jobs to record stores closing their doors,' Cary Sherman, president of the Recording Industry Association of America (RIAA), said in a statement. 'Songlifting is against the law, and breaking the law must carry consequences' (*The Star Tribune*)

Attack of the Snowclones

A freshly minted word, **snowclone,** gives a name to a phenomenon that has been around for some time: a well-known phrase that is altered and reused.

The 'classic' snowclone, which gives the phenomenon its name, is 'If the Eskimos [or, as culturally sensitive snowcloners would have it, the Inuit] have *N* words for snow, then *X* must have *Y* words for *Z*'. This can be adapted again and again, with *Eskimos, words,* and *snow* all being replaced, as well as the other variables. This leaves us with a kind of 'ghost sentence', in which the faint outlines of the long-dead original are still visible in the new construction.

Film straplines are fair game for snowcloning, with one of the best examples being the slogan for the 1979 film *Alien:* 'In space, no-one can hear you scream', which becomes 'In *X*, no-one can hear you *Y*'.

But it's fashion that has spawned the most widespread snowclone of all: '*X* is the new *Y*', which began life as 'brown is the new black'. Here are some examples from the Collins Word Web, our vast database of real English usage:

Peace is the new war; property is the new porn; Glasgow is the new black; bleak is the new black; cheap is the new chic; sixty is the new fifty; together is the new alone; black is the new black; sleep is the new sex; fit is the new rich; comedy is the new rock 'n' roll; fish is the new rock 'n' roll; soup is the new black; staying in is the new going out; celibacy is the new deviance. And finally, inevitably, *black is the new brown.*

sorbet sex *n.* a casual sexual relationship undertaken in the period between two more serious relationships [first used in the HBO TV series *Sex and the City*; the analogy is of a palate-cleansing sorbet during a multiple-course meal.]

> 'Sorbet sex stops me obsessing when I meet someone else that I like, because I've got another point of comparison besides my ex and it stops me fantasizing about him,' says my girlfriend Amy, who recently found herself in the sack with a friend after breaking up with her boyfriend (*The Independent*)

spam rage *n.* aggressive behaviour by a computer user in reaction to spam (junk e-mail) [modelled on ROAD RAGE]

> But spam rage, like road and air rage, has pushed others to extremes in their battle against unwarranted e-mail. Some people spend hours tracking spammers and reporting them to authorities. Others engage in cyberwarfare by shutting down spammers' Web pages or putting spammers' addresses on Web sites. Others sue. A few resort to threats (*USA Today*)

sping *n.* an electronic update sent to a central server or website by a splog (spam blog) rather than a genuine blog when the splog is updated [a blend of SPAM and PING: the latter representing the imagined sound of an electronic update arriving]. *See also* **splog**

> Just as e-mail is overcome by spam, the blogosphere is sullied by splogs and spings. The influx of spam-related blogs accounts for nine percent of new blogs (*ClickZ News*)

spit *n.* unsolicited commercial communications received on a telephone linked to the internet [an acronym of SPAM OVER INTERNET TELEPHONY]

> A new plague of unwanted messages threatens internet users, according to a US company. Spam and spim – spam by instant messenger – are about to be joined by 'spit' – spam over internet telephony. Qovia, based in Frederick, Maryland, have recently filed two patent applications for technology to thwart spit. Internet telephony involves making phone calls using the internet instead of traditional phone lines. Also known as voice-over IP (VoIP), it is rapidly rising in popularity thanks to the fact that internet connections are becoming faster, and because it is cheap – it avoids the taxes levied on landline calls (*New Scientist*)

splog *n.* a blog that contains little or no content from the owner, but merely links to affiliated commercial websites [a blend of SPAM and BLOG]

> There are millions of spam blogs – or 'splogs' – with more added every day. And they aren't going away. 'It's not getting any better and it's probably getting worse,' says Tim Finin, a computer science professor

at University of Maryland, Baltimore County, who
helped write a paper about detecting splogs that was
presented last month at an American Association for
Artificial Intelligence conference (*InformationWeek*)

squeaky-bum time *n. British, soccer, informal* a tense situation, esp the final stages of a league competition [coined by Sir Alex Ferguson (born 1941) in an attempt to convey the nervous tension experienced by those involved]

It's that time again. Squeaky-bum time. And
Manchester United boss Alex Ferguson expects all the
uncomfortable noises to come from Chelsea (*The Sun*)

stagflation *n. jocular* the process by which stag weekends have become increasingly elaborate and expensive [a blend of STAG and (IN)FLATION; echoing the financial term *stagflation* (a blend of STAG(NATION) and (IN)FLATION), which was coined by UK Conservative MP and *Spectator* editor Ian MacLeod in 1965]

How times have changed. The stag night is like the
red squirrel, a much-loved and respectable native
creature giving way to an invasion of bigger exotic
varieties, the stag weekend and even week. This is the
era of 'stagflation', with the average stag weekend
costing £365 a head, according to a 2004 Morgan

starchitect *n.* *informal* a well-known and well-paid architect noted for his or her landmark buildings [a blend of STAR and ARCHITECT] > **starchitecture** *n.*

> Call it the Bilbao effect – 'starchitects' who can single-handedly put cities on the world stage, as US designer Frank Gehry did with his warped silver Guggenheim museum for Bilbao, Spain. It's yet another sign of architecture increasing its grip on the image and identity of world cities (*The Australian*)

stealth disco *n.* the act of disco dancing or playing air guitar behind an unsuspecting person, usually while being filmed for broadcast on the internet

> Stealth disco – the gentle art of surreptitious dance in the work place. Get down and watch the hilarious video! (*evilpundit.com*)

stoozing *n.* *informal* the practice of taking advantage of the introductory interest-free period offered by a credit-card company to borrow money for investing profitably elsewhere > **stooze** *vb.* [from *Stooz*, the nickname of a person who has offered online advice on this practice]

> As the number of 0% cards has increased, so has the number of people taking advantage. Perhaps the most

popular name for it is 'stoozing', which is usually used
to describe any technique to profit out of playing
credit card companies' deals (*moneysavingexpert.com*)

strategic philanthropy *n.* the practice among
businesses of seeking to make only charitable
donations that will somehow be good for business

> It is part of a broad, historic shift in the nature of
> corporate philanthropy. It goes by a variety of names –
> strategic philanthropy, cause marketing, values-led
> marketing, or just plain corporate citizenship – but
> what is happening here is clear: In an attempt to
> become more strategic in their philanthropy,
> corporate donors are tying their gifts more closely to
> their company's business objectives, according to a
> special investigative article in the Summer 2005 issue
> of the Stanford Social Innovation Review
> (*businesswire.com*)

tanorexic *adj.* **1** *informal* obsessed with having a
permanent deep tan and compelled to use tanning
machines more than is healthy │ *n.* **2** a tanorexic
person [a blend of TAN and ANOREXIC]

> … a 28-year-old law student from Glasgow, is a typical
> tanorexic. 'I go on the sunbed three times a week in
> summer and five times a week in winter. I love the
> feeling it gives me. It's like an infusion of brightness
> and warmth and light. No question about it, I look
> much healthier with a tan.' In truth, she does not look

that great. Her skin is a luminous hazelnut brown and has a leathery texture *(The Times)*

tart fuel *n. derogatory, slang* alcopops collectively, seen as being the drink of choice of young women

> A friend of mine still insists that beer is more fattening than alcopops (what I fondly refer to as tart fuel) – it's his humble opinion that drinking one beer is the equivalent to eating two loaves of bread *(News24.com)*

technocoolie *n. informal* an IT worker in the developing world who works on products or services that are sold in the West [a blend of TECHNOLOGY and COOLIE]

> As the Indian IT industry matures and gains global acceptance, academic institutions need to be geared to produce 'technocrats' and not 'technocoolies' says Prashant Govil *(expressitpeople.com)*

text stalking *or* **textual harassment** *n. informal* harassment by the sending of unwanted or threatening text messages

> The rise of so called 'text stalking' – often committed by vengeful former boyfriends – is causing particular alarm, with victims hit by threatening words or pictures dozens of times in a single day *(The Independent on Sunday)*

Winning wordsmiths

English has a huge vocabulary, larger than any other language. Much of this owes to the fact that English is a hybrid of the Germanic (Old English) and the Romance (Norman French). Successive waves of immigration have enriched our vocabulary further, while the British Empire facilitated the cheerful looting of far-flung languages. But individual writers have also expanded our linguistic horizons.

The obvious example is William Shakespeare, who introduced a wealth of words and phrases, including *ill-starred, lacklustre, salad days, besmirch,* and *fashionable.* Less well known, but almost as influential, was the seventeenth-century author Sir Thomas Browne, who contributed words such as *antediluvian* and *electricity.* Edmund Spenser had already made his mark in 1596, with *blatant* in *The Faerie Queen.* With *Gulliver's Travels* in 1726, Jonathan Swift gave us *Lilliputian, Brobdingnagian,* and *yahoo.* Horace Walpole invented the word *serendipity* in 1754 to describe the faculty of making fortunate discoveries by accident, as displayed in the Persian fairy tale *The Three Princes of Serendip.* Samuel Taylor Coleridge created the word *intensify* to describe the effects of opium. And Lewis Carroll bequeathed *chortle* and *galumph* to the language in his 1871 nonsense poem *Jabberwocky.*

The phenomenon shows no sign of losing steam. Harry Potter author JK Rowling provides *quidditch* and *Muggle.* And Canadian novelist Douglas Coupland has had a particularly marked impact with *Generation X* and *McJob.*

theocon *n. US* a person with conservative views who believes that religion, esp Christianity, should be the dominant influence in government policy [a blend of THEOCRAT and CON(SERVATIVE): modelled on NEOCON]

> If you're one of those unhappy people who feel compelled to follow the burps and gurgles of the US political debate, you will have noticed the recent introduction of a new word. The term 'theocon' is suddenly everywhere. Worse, 'theocons' themselves are suddenly everywhere – or so we are supposed to think (*Bloomberg*)

thinspiration *n.* pictures of underweight people used as inspirational material by anorexics who believe that anorexia is a lifestyle choice rather than a disorder [a blend of THIN and INSPIRATION]. *See also* **pro-ana, pro-mia**

> Type 'pro-ana' into any Internet search engine and you'll get a disturbing glimpse into a deadly obsession with thin. There are websites with 'thinspiration' photo galleries of waif-thin models and famous celebrities with eating disorders like Mary-Kate Olsen and Karen Carpenter (*healthyplace.com*)

thumb generation *or* **thumb tribe** *n. informal* the generation of young people who have grown up with mobile phones and video games, and have developed an unusual degree of strength and versatility in their thumbs as a result [a direct translation of the Japanese *oya yubi sedai*]. *See* **Mob rule, page 94**

> In Japan, the trend was particularly marked. Plant even found the under-25s referred to themselves as *oya yubi sedai* – the thumb generation, or thumb tribe. As their thumbs become stronger and more dexterous, Plant found that the thumb tribe is using its favourite digit for other tasks that are traditionally the finger's job, such as pointing at things or ringing doorbells (*The Observer*)

ticking-bomb scenario *n.* a hypothetical situation used in discussions of the ethics of torture; in this situation, a terrorist has planted a hidden timebomb that will explode with substantial loss of life unless he or she is tortured into revealing its location

> The 'ticking-bomb' scenario, as it is usually known, can seem persuasive. If someone knows of a vast bomb primed to explode in the heart of central London, how could one not torture him, to save thousands of lives? Exposed to reality, however, the hypothetical is no longer so neat. It has damaging consequences for individuals and societies alike (*Prospect*)

tiger kidnapping *n.* *informal* the practice, employed by some terrorists and criminals in Northern Ireland, of forcing a person to commit a crime while his or family is held captive

> The gang then surprises the person at home and takes them at gunpoint to their business premises where the victim hands over takings. Tiger kidnapping is effective: using this method, a gang can net up to 10 times more than in a conventional robbery, says Brian Cremin, of Crime Management Group, a consultancy firm specialising in crime risk (*The Times*)

tigger *vb. informal* to damage (electronic equipment) esp as a result of tinkering [perhaps after the rumbustious character 'Tigger' in AA Milne's *The House at Pooh Corner* (1928); influenced by BUGGER] > **tiggered** *adj.*

> Italian senators opening attachments promising gay porn have tiggered the government's computer system (*The Inquirer*)

tiktaalik *n. Tiktaalik roseae,* an extinct species discovered in 2006 that is believed to be the missing link between water and land animals [from the Inuktitut word for a large freshwater fish or burbot]. *See also* **fishapod.** *See* **Mix and match, page 59**

> Culture-war observers might note that Tiktaalik bears a weird resemblance to the Darwin fish – the pictogram of a two-legged creature that parodies the

ichthus symbol used by devout Christians. The coincidence is particularly poignant, given that Tiktaalik has re-emerged at a dismal moment for Christian fundamentalists and other opponents of evolutionary biology (*The Wall Street Journal*)

tinkerman *n. chiefly British, sport, esp soccer, informal* a manager or coach who continually experiments by changing the personnel or formation of a team from game to game [originally a nickname given to Claudio Ranieri (born 1951), manager of Chelsea FC 2000–2004, but now more generally applied]

In discarding the midfield formation that has served England adequately for much of the qualifying campaign, Eriksson is either conducting an astute experiment before the trials his team may face later in the tournament or displaying a tinkerman's touch before a momentous fixture (*The Times*)

toad juice *n. Australian* a fertilizer produced by liquidizing cane toads

Even a plan by the conservation group FrogWatch to turn toad carcasses into liquid fertiliser (Toad Juice) is unlikely to make a dent. Cane toads, introduced in the 1930s to kill insect pests in sugar canefields, have spread from coastal Queensland to within 40 kilometres of Darwin. They have become one of Australia's most serious ecological disasters (*The Age*)

Textual intercourse

Text messaging, or SMS (short message service) to give it its technical name, was the surprise hit amongst the few functions that early mobile phones offered. Phone manufacturers thought it would be of little interest, and were taken aback by the speed with which we took to thumbing our keypads. A distinct *textspeak* soon evolved, with messages like 'cu l8r' and 'wot u up 2 2nite m8?' universally understood.

This brought on a moral panic, with rumours of children unable to read normal English and the possibility of exam boards allowing test papers to be written in textspeak to cater to the **thumb generation.** But the fuss over textspeak seems largely misplaced. While text messages continue to be **disemvowelled,** most other forms of writing preserve the traditional rules of spelling, grammar, and punctuation.

When Martin Amis's novel *Yellow Dog* appeared in 2003, for example, critics were quick to point out that his use of textspeak in email exchanges rang false. When we send texts, we're keen on keeping them as short as possible, but with the luxury of a keyboard rather than a keypad, we prefer the long way round.

This phenomenon holds true even in the cut and thrust of internet forums. There's no easier way to draw flames than to trot out messages in textspeak or **leet** – 'Write properly! Are you eight years old?' – and many sites have FAQs encouraging the use of 'proper' English. Textspeak may flourish in SMS and in juvenile chatrooms, but generally it's the comfort and clarity of conventional language that wins through.

tombstoning *n. British, slang* the activity of diving off cliffs into the sea [so called because of the potential danger involved]

> Cornish coastguards have renewed their warning about 'tombstoning' following another accident on Thursday evening ... John Rossiter from Falmouth coastguards said: 'It really is a very dangerous game. 'People are just not sure of the depth of the water and they're toppling over and striking their heads and limbs on rocks. 'We ask people to please think about it. It's just far too dangerous' (*BBC News*)

toolie *n. Australian, slang* an adult who gatecrashes the 'Schoolies' celebrations marking the end of school leavers' final-year exams, especially one making sexual advances towards students [a blend of TOOL (slang for penis or a contemptible person) and SCHOOLIE]

> His biggest gripe with last year's Schoolies festival was the ease with which 'toolies' could obtain ID tags. The tags, which are worn around the wrist, identify an individual as a genuine schoolie. 'When we went up to get one they didn't ask for a school ID or anything. You just said who you were, showed a bankcard or whatever and had a witness to say that it was true,' he said (*The Courier-Mail*)

toyetic *adj.* (of a film or television programme) having the potential to spin off profitable merchandise such as toys, computer games, etc

> Bob's 'can-do' attitude turned out to have strong
> appeal in North America. Another element in Bob's
> American success is that he has turned out to be what
> media analysts now term 'toyetic' … Publishers,
> television companies, and those in the intellectual
> property rights business are increasingly concerned
> with how well children's characters will translate into
> toys for the American market. Scots author and
> illustrator Debi Gliori was once dissuaded from
> writing a book about badgers on the basis that
> 'Americans don't do badgers' (*The Herald*)

transfer tube *n.* a body bag [the phrase is often cited
as an example of the current US administration's
alleged tendency to coin euphemisms to gloss over
unpleasant things, but is more likely to have arisen
from a corruption of the term *transfer case*, which is
used by the US military to refer to the metal cases in
which bodies are transported]

> The US Defence Department has forbidden the media
> from filming returns of 'transfer tubes' (the latest
> euphemism for body bags) lest such images disturb
> the public (*The Globe and Mail*)

trauma pod *n.* a proposed remote-controlled robot
that can perform surgical procedures on wounded
soldiers on the battlefield

The Pentagon is awarding $12 million in grants to develop unmanned 'trauma pod' robots to perform full scalpel-and-stitch surgeries on wounded soldiers in battlefield conditions. Researchers have prepared a futuristic 'concept video,' showing with full color and sound effects the notion that robots in unmanned vehicles can operate on soldiers under enemy fire and then evacuate them (*Wired*)

Trojan duck *n.* *informal* a duck that carries avian flu and is therefore a threat to other birds and also to humans, but which shows no outward signs of infection [modelled on TROJAN HORSE]

'Trojan ducks' could trigger a global Asian flu pandemic, say scientists … An analysis of H5N1 influenza in ducks in Asia has disclosed that since 2002 the strain has become much less dangerous to the birds, allowing them to become a reservoir for the disease (*The Times*)

trust economy *n.* the trust-based system on which many websites and web-based exchanges operate

Wikis, for example, are a perfect example of the 'trust economy', a space in which the exchange of ideas and information depends almost entirely on a high degree of trust between all the participants (*BBC Online*)

truthiness *n.* *informal* the quality of being what someone wishes or feels to be true, regardless of the facts [coined by US comedian Stephen Colbert in late 2005 to combine TRUTH with a sense of vagueness or approximation; the term existed earlier as an obscure synonym for TRUTHFULNESS]

> He calls his show a 'no-fact zone' and he plays a blowhard anchor, what he calls a 'high-status idiot,' an unread, grotesque bully who lives on 'truthiness,' a Colbert word for faith in what you believe to be true rather than what is true. He promises not to tell you the truth 'but to feel the truth at you.' (*vivelecanada.ca*)

tryvertising *n.* a form of marketing in which consumers are allowed to use products free of charge for a period of time [a blend of TRY and ADVERTISING]

> In its latest edition the online magazine *Trendspotting* sums up the difference in approach between sampling and what it calls 'tryvertising', pointing to Gillette Australia's giveaway last April of 2.2 million of its new disposable Brush-Ups™ teeth cleaners – the largest one-day sampling ever in Australia – and Gillette's decision to give the product to KLM airline passengers after their meal (*The Sydney Morning Herald*)

Twenty20 *n.* a form of one-day cricket in which each side bats for twenty overs

> Who knows when last, if ever, *The Times* used three exclamation marks on its front page. That institution

of the British press was moved to extreme
punctuation on a front-page banner: 'Aussies
thrashed!!!' That was nothing compared with the orgy
of triumph in other papers at England's Twenty20 win
over Australia. It was as if the Ashes were as good as
won. 'You Sheilas,' screamed The Daily Mirror,
claiming, 'We Won the Bashes'. The Sun crowed,
'Thrashes' and 'Oz left in Rooins' (*Northern Territory
News*)

ubersexual *n.* a man who exhibits traditional
masculine qualities as well as the caring nature of the
'New Man' [modelled on METROSEXUAL: a
heterosexual man who spends a lot of time and money
on his appearance and likes to shop]

Ubersexuals aren't just clothes horses but can
multitask – you will find your average ubersexual
pleasuring his woman while changing a nappy and
conversing intelligently about the new Rubens
exhibition (*The Guardian*)

uniname *n.* a single name for a celebrity couple that
combines elements of their individual names [UNI- +
NAME]

We asked readers to create a celebrity couple with a
cool combined name that puts Brangelina to shame.
The duos you came up with (Anna Nicole Smith and
Mel Brooks? Could happen!) were as funny as the
uninames (*Chicago Tribune*)

Titles in tandem

The one-word moniker has long been popular with two social groups resistant to the idea of anything as cumbersome and mediocre as a surname: musical super-divas and South American footballers (think Madonna and Pele). Over the past few years, however, the term **uniname** has sprung into being to describe the combined names given to certain famous couples by ingenious media wordsmiths. It started in the early noughties with the high-profile relationship of Ben Affleck and Jennifer Lopez. Their media-friendly love affair, broadcast to the masses in film and song, earned the couple the epithet *Bennifer*. This blending of first names served a dual purpose: firstly, as useful shorthand for referring to the couple and their activities; and secondly, as a virtual brand name, emphasizing their fame. Not every celebrity couple is eligible for this accolade. There has to be a clever way of blending the two names into one. This can be done using rhyme (as in *Bennifer*), assonance (*Brangelina* – Brad Pitt and Angelina Jolie), punning (*TomKat* – Tom Cruise and Katie Holmes), or simply the combining of one part of each name into an easily pronounced word (*Wayleen* – Wayne Rooney and Colleen McLoughlin).

Although not strictly conforming to the conventions of the uniname (note the conjunction in the middle), the Posh'n'Becks brand of David Beckham and his spicy wife Victoria is strongly enough established in British English to have become rhyming slang: *posh'n'becks* = *sex*.

user tagging *n.* a system that allows website users to share their internet bookmarks and the labels ('tags') that they have attached to those sites

> User tagging is emerging as a major organizational tool on the Web as it allows users to organize and navigate results easily and clearly using intelligent groupings for increased collaboration (*Business Wire*)

vanity editing *n.* the act of editing a page of a wiki site to provide a more favourable commentary on oneself or one's company, etc

> He has faced claims of vanity editing for making changes to an entry on podcasting: a technology that he had a significant role in developing. The claim – and his response to it (that he accidentally edited out part of the entry while experimenting with the wiki interface) – has prompted debate among Wikipedia editors and an update to his own Wikipedia page (*The Guardian*)

vlog *n.* a video journal filmed using a camcorder, webcam, or mobile phone and placed on the internet [a blend of VIDEO and BLOG] > **vlogger** *n.* > **vlogging** *n.*

> It was inevitable: Bloggers who previously wrote endlessly about everything from politics to tech tips to how to fry an egg on a hot sidewalk can now take their commentary, advice and random experiments to the

next level by filming and broadcasting their work, thanks to the latest web trend – video blogging. Video blogs – also known by their shorter, clunkier name, vlogs – are blogs that primarily feature video shorts instead of text (*Wired*)

VOD *abbreviation for* video on demand: an interactive television system which allows viewers to select content and view it at a time of their own choosing

Television has come a long way from the simple broadcasting of a handful of channels. Now the telly can offer hundreds of choices as well as interactive quizzes, games and voting. But TV continues to evolve and the next big thing set to hit European screens could be video on demand (VOD). VOD allows viewers to call up TV shows, films and sport just by pushing a few buttons on their remote control. The difference from current on-demand offers … is that VOD programmes can be ordered and viewed immediately and they have full VCR functionality. It is like having a DVD but without having to go to the video shop (*The Guardian*)

vodcasting *n.* the creation and provision of video files for download to a computer, MP3 player, etc. > **vodcast** *n, vb. See also* **VOD, vlog** [from VOD + -CASTING; modelled on PODCASTING, itself modelled on BROADCASTING]

It's still early days for podcasting, and one trend to

watch out for will be the growing emergence of video podcasting, known as vlogging or vodcasting (*The Sydney Morning Herald*)

voice-lift *n.* a cosmetic surgical operation on the vocal cords to make the voice sound younger

> After the tummy tuck, the forehead tightener, the nose job and the jowl trim, something still might be giving away your age: your voice. For patients who think their trembly, raspy or wispy words don't match their newly firm face and figure, there's a procedure that claims to make them sound younger too: the voice lift (*Canada.com*)

voluntourism *n.* a form of tourism in which travellers undertake voluntary work to help communities or the environment in the places they are visiting [a blend of VOLUNTEER and TOURISM]

> Voluntourism seems to have eclipsed the long-established, but less glamorous, business of sponsoring a child overseas (*The Times*)

vuvuzela *n. South African* an elongated plastic instrument that football fans blow to make a loud noise similar to the trumpeting of an elephant [from Zulu]

> While the blaring sounds of the vuvuzela signal sports victories, for residents of Naledi Extension in Soweto

it means the streets are safe to walk. The vuvuzela is
the clarion call of the 'Vietnams', a group of
volunteers who patrol the streets from dawn to dusk
in their crackdown on criminals *(The Star)*

Wag *n. informal* the wife or girlfriend of a famous
sportsman, esp during a tournament [the singular is a
back formation from an acronym for *w(ives) a(nd)
g(irlfriends)*]

> The England Wags have strength in depth, especially
> when it comes to drinking. They can break swiftly for
> a party, often late into the night after normal time.
> When under pressure – perhaps with nothing else to
> do during the day – their defensive shopping is
> second to none *(The Sunday Times)*

washable computing *or* **wearable computing** *n.* a
fabric that contains microchips and conductive fibres
that enable microcomputers to be installed in it;
clothing made of such a fabric

> Electrospinning is compatible with the needs of
> washable computing because it deposits a permeable
> mesh, rather than a solid, impermeable layer (as
> would silk-screening or printing) *(research.ibm.com)*

waterhog *n. informal* a person who uses water
selfishly or irresponsibly, esp at a time of water
shortage

Our clement weather means we should keep an out eye for a new species of pig – the waterhog. This is not a marsh-loving relation to Africa's sharp-tusked warthog but the latest twist in the hosepipe ban saga. Three Valleys Water has posted a form on its website that allows its customer to report any 'irresponsible water user' – aka 'waterhog' – in their community (*The Guardian*)

Web 2.0 *n.* the internet in its current or near-future state in which interactive experience plays a more important role than simply accessing information; this includes web forums, blogs, wikis, etc

It's a fundamental change. What started as a simple way for people to retrieve information, and then became a huge information depository, has evolved into something completely new – Web 2.0. Previously people were just consuming information off the web, but now they go to the internet to participate, to communicate, to contribute. Whereas we used to access the internet from a personal computer at work or home, we now expect to have access wherever we go (*Melbourne Herald Sun*)

webisode *n.* an episode of a video or television series that is available online for viewing or download

NBC is also developing a raft of online and interactive components for a number of its television properties, including webisodes from *The Office* and the new drama *Friday Night Lights* (*World Screen News*)

The frontiers of knowledge

One obvious reason for our ever-expanding vocabulary is that as we discover more about the universe, we need more words to describe it. The honour of naming new phenomena usually falls to the scientists who discover them, and thus the scientific community has harboured a great many neologists over the centuries. Scientists who do make their mark on the language join the distinguished company of Sir Isaac Newton, who coined *centrifugal* in 1687.

Most new scientific terms are built from existing elements, usually in Latin or Greek. Thus *dinosaur* – 'terrible lizard' – was coined by British anatomist Richard Owen in 1841. Others, however, mix linguistic roots or draw on imaginative sources. The word *gene* was backformed by Danish botanist Wilhelm Johannsen in 1911, from *genetics,* providing the model for Richard Dawkins' *meme* in 1976. *Quark,* meaning a subatomic particle, takes its name from a nonsense word in James Joyce's 1939 novel *Finnegans Wake*; Murray Gell-Mann demonstrating that at least some scientists have literary inclinations.

Not all scientific terms catch on, however, even when they denote their subject with admirable precision. The sixteenth-century medical writer Dr Edward Strother coined the word *aequeosalinocalcalinosetaceoaluminosocupreovitriolic* to describe the spa waters at Bath. Strangely, this one isn't on the tips of most people's tongues, even in Bath itself!

Wellywood *n.* *New Zealand, informal* Wellington, the capital city of New Zealand, considered as a centre of filmmaking [a blend of WELLINGTON and HOLLYWOOD]

> 'Wellywood' as the locals like to call it, was the base for the trilogy's filming studios. Mount Victoria's City Belt was transformed into Hobbiton Woods; the Gondorian city of Minas Tirith and the fortifications of Helms Deep were created just off State Highway 2 and Kaitoke Regional Park, just north of the city, was the elvish realm of Rivendell (*The Sydney Morning Herald*)

were-rabbit *n.* *British* a giant rabbit reported to be devastating Northumberland allotments in April 2006 [named after the monster in the animated film *Wallace and Gromit: the Curse of the Were-Rabbit* (2005); modelled on WEREWOLF]

> The predator, which has been nicknamed the were-rabbit because of its similarity to the hungry bunny in the recent Wallace and Gromit film, is described as being black and brown and much bigger than either a hare or a rabbit. One of its ears is also said to be noticeably large than the other. 'It's a monster,' said one of the guards charged with terminating the rabbit (*The Guardian*)

whorgy *n.* *slang* an occasion on which a man has

180

sexual intercourse with several women [a blend of WHORE and ORGY]

> When a man has sex with several women, it is usually known as a reverse gang bang or a whorgy. (*passion.com*)

wiki *n.* **1** a website, or part of one, whose content can be edited by anyone who visits it **2** *as modifier wiki technology* [from Hawaiian *wiki-wiki* quick, coined by Ward Cunningham (born 1949), the US programmer who invented the concept]

> Most encyclopedias start to fossilize the moment they're printed on a page. But add wiki software and you get something self-repairing and almost alive (*Wired*)

wikispam *n.* commercial links or endorsements posted on a wiki site for purposes of advertising, contrary to the purposes for which the wiki was established [from WIKI + SPAM]

> A few fellow edtech bloggers who have taken up wikis have of late been inundated by wikispam. I too was pelted almost continuously with wikispam from China from around June through to September when I finally screamed enough! (*edtechpost.ca*)

wikitorial *n.* an online newspaper or magazine

editorial that can be altered by readers using open-source editing technology [a blend of WIKI and EDITORIAL]

> We begin with just one wikitorial. Maybe a year from now a link for 'wiki this page' will be as common on the Web as 'printer-friendly' or 'e-mail this article.' Or maybe not (*Los Angeles Times*)

> LA Times 'wikitorial' gives editors red faces: It was the boldest of innovations. A chance for the mainstream media to strike back against the upstarts of the online world. On Friday the Los Angeles Times – an unwieldy broadsheet newspaper – launched its 'wikitorial', an interactive device allowing readers to contribute to and rewrite its editorial column … But by Sunday, readers were met with the following statement: 'Where is the wikitorial? Unfortunately, we have had to remove this feature, at least temporarily, because a few readers were flooding the site with inappropriate material' (*The Guardian*)

wristband generation *n. British* The age-group that is accustomed to demonstrating support of charitable causes by wearing coloured wristbands or bracelets

> If Cameron's Tories want to chase the 'wristband generation' of younger voters, might they decide to join Greenpeace (whose protestors recently mucked up Mr Blair's CBI speech) and oppose nuclear power? (*themanufacturer.com*)

yeppies *pl n, sing.* **yeppy** *informal* people in their twenties or early thirties who are reluctant to commit to a career, partner, or parenthood until they have tried a variety of lifestyles [from *y(oung) e(xperimenting) p(erfection) s(eekers)*; modelled on YUPPIE]

> They are twentysomething, ambitious and confused. And they won't commit to anything until they are certain it will bring them enduring happiness. Meet the 'Young Experimenting Perfection Seekers' – Yeppies, as anthropologists are calling them (*The Observer*)

yindie *n. informal* a person in his or her twenties or early thirties who combines a lucrative career with non-mainstream tastes [a blend of YUPPIE and INDIE]

> Not since the 1980s, when the Yuppie was king, have we encountered such a powerful social group. They've been around for a few years, but only now have they been comprehensively nailed. Meet the Yindie: half-yuppie, half-indie, moneyed urban hipsters aged 20–35 who listen to wry northern indie music on their iPod nanos,™ and who think Zadie Smith is the pinnacle of alternative fiction (*The Independent*)

yupster *n. informal* an affluent person with a preference for the sort of independent music that was previously the preserve of dedicated fans [a blend of

YUPPIE and HIPSTER; the term was earlier used as a variant of YUPPIE]

> 'This year, there's a real consensus around 10 records,' says Adam Shore of Vice Recordings. 'And they're all this type of indie rock.' Connoisseurs are crediting 'Yupsters' – Yuppie hipsters – for the change … For the past decade, indie records sold primarily to obsessives because, without major-label distribution, the music was tough to find. But now a few clicks and an iPod™ are all it takes for would-be Yupsters to indulge any curiosity (*Newsweek*)

Yurp *n. facetious* a satirical term for Europe as perceived by right-wing US politicians [an approximation of George W Bush's pronunciation of EUROPE]

> Not that the Bushies would be too discomforted by that. In fact, this scene – Gore feted by bien pensant European elitists – would confirm everything they like to believe about Gore and his fellow Democrats: that they might be popular with the cheese-eating surrender monkeys of Yurp, but they're woefully out of touch at home (*The Guardian*)